SHOULD THE BLAME for outbreak of war in 1939 be handed to ex-Corporal Hitler, or to the 'peacemakers' of World War One? Or perhaps responsibility goes further back to the unfinished business of 1914, interrupted by the irrelevant war which settled nothing. Or perhaps even older traditional European disagreements, suspicions and arguments were involved.

Using carefully edited documents from all major sources, this book examines possible origins and combinations of origins of World War Two; the legacy of World War One, the German grievances, the personality and power of Hitler, the cult of Nazism, the ambitions of Japan. Hitler is placed in the context of his time. Important controversies are considered—the harsh terms of the Paris peace treaty, the German violation of the disarmament clauses, Chamberlain and Munich, British unpreparedness for war. Events leading to war are described against their wider background; the Russian upheavals, Japanese imperialism, European war weariness, British pacificism, and the development in Nazi Germany of the means of mobile conflict and *blitzkrieg* which were to explode war from the static, bloody, trenches of 1914–18, that 'war to end all wars'.

Illustrated throughout, this new volume in the WAYLAND DOCUMENTARY HISTORY SERIES contributes valuable background reading for the period.

Frontispiece Hitler addresses new members of the Hitler Youth Movement in Munich (November, 1934)

The Origins of World War Two

by Roger Parkinson

WAYLAND PUBLISHERS LONDON

*Available in hardback (*limp edition also available):*

THE VIKINGS   Michael Gibson
*MEDIEVAL PILGRIMS   Alan Kendall
THE BLACK DEATH AND PEASANTS' REVOLT   Leonard Cowie
*THE REFORMATION OF THE SIXTEENTH CENTURY   Leonard Cowie
THE PILGRIM FATHERS   Leonard Cowie
*WITCHCRAFT   Roger Hart
*PLAGUE AND FIRE   Leonard Cowie
*THE AGE OF DICKENS   Patrick Rooke
ENGLAND EXPECTS   Roger Hart
GLADSTONE AND DISRAELI   Patrick Rooke
*ORIGINS OF WORLD WAR ONE   R. Parkinson
THE GREAT DEPRESSION   Marion Yass
THE THIRD REICH   Michael Berwick
*ORIGINS OF WORLD WAR TWO   R. Parkinson
*THE HOME FRONT   Marion Yass
HIROSHIMA   Marion Yass
WOMEN'S RIGHTS   Patrick Rooke
THE COLD WAR   Elisabeth Barker
THE TRIAL AND EXECUTION OF CHARLES I   Leonard Cowie
BLACK CARGO   Richard Howard
RUSSIA UNDER STALIN   Michael Gibson
THE BRITISH RAJ   Denis Judd
ITALY UNDER MUSSOLINI   Christopher Leeds
THE RISE OF JAPAN   Michael Gibson

SBN (hardback edition): 85340 014 8
SBN (limp edition): 85340 212 4
Fourth impression 1976
Copyright © 1970 by Wayland (Publishers) Ltd
49 Lansdowne Place, Hove, Sussex BN3 1HS
Printed in Great Britain by
The Garden City Press Limited, Letchworth, Hertfordshire SG6 1JS

Contents

The Illustrations

Introduction

IN 1918 THE Western World lay bleeding and exhausted after the greatest catastrophe it had ever experienced. Four major Empires—Russia, Germany, Austria–Hungary, Turkey—had collapsed. Nations had been split and the former economic structures were in shreds.

Exhausted world

Yet World War One had settled nothing. The basic problems of Europe remained and had even been aggravated by the massive convulsion of conflict. Germany still felt encircled, France still felt threatened by Germany.

World War One had been fought to make the world safe for democracy and for small nations, declared President Wilson. From the very start, the invasion of Serbia and Belgium had made small-state independence an inherent war issue. This independence issue became a major factor in the peacemaking process. Small nations were created from old Empires and given democratic rule. But they were flimsy, vulnerable—and potential sources of renewed conflict.

New nations

The creation of these nations reflected the hopes of the victors. The war had been fought which would end all wars. The task of the peacemakers was to translate this idealism into the terms of peace and into international affairs. President Wilson's famous 'Fourteen Points' of 1917 and other optimistic declarations of principles by the Allies were used as the basis. (Extracts from the Fourteen Points appear at the end of this Chapter.)

And yet America, after putting her hand into European affairs and drawing it out again bloody, retired once more into her own Continent. President Wilson, after insisting on the importance of

American isolation

9

Opposite Hitler the young soldier (middle); only the piercing eyes and clenched chin give a hint of the future Führer

his Points, and after insisting that the equally idealistic Covenant of the League of Nations should form the first part of the Treaty of Versailles, over-estimated his support at home. The Treaty was signed on 28 June 1919. In November, the American Congress refused to ratify the Covenant. Wilson was desperately disappointed.

In 1920 the Anglo–American guarantee to protect France was invalidated. Europe was to be left alone, to go her own way, until 1941.

Battle for
peace

But this Europe badly needed help. There were to be no more wars, said the optimists. Yet in Russia, Trotsky was saying: 'The working class of the Soviet Union will become the imitator of the liquidation of capitalism on a global scale.' The war with Germany was over, yet the militants were crying: 'Hang the Kaiser!' and 'Make the Huns pay!' The war had been fought by a multitude of peoples. Now they all clamoured for a say in the peace.

War was over. But already, there seemed too many problems for peace to battle with.

Wilson's
Fourteen
Points

PRESIDENT WILSON'S FOURTEEN POINTS
These principles, announced by President Wilson on 8 January 1918 constituted the American war aims. They were later elaborated by Wilson with his 'Four Principles', 11 February 1918, 'Four Ends', 4 July 1918 and 'Five Particulars', 27 September 1918:

'An open
peace'

'(1) Open covenants of peace openly arrived at . . . there shall be no private international understandings of any kind, but diplomacy shall proceed always frankly and in the public view.

'(2) Absolute freedom of navigation upon the seas, outside territorial waters, alike in peace and in war, except as the seas may be closed in whole or in part by international action for the enforcement of international covenants.

'(3) The removal, so far as possible, of all economic barriers . . . the establishment of an equality of trade conditions among all the nations consenting to the peace and associating themselves for its maintenance.

'(4) Adequate guarantees given and taken that national armaments will be reduced to the lowest point consistent with domestic safety.

'(5) A free, open-minded, and absolutely impartial adjustment of all colonial claims, based upon a strict observance of the principle that in determining all such questions of sovereignty the interests of the populations concerned must have equal weight with the equitable claims of the government whose title is to be determined.

'(6) The evacuation of all Russian territory and such a settlement *Russia* of all questions affecting Russia as will secure the best and freest co-operation of the other nations of the world in obtaining for her an unhampered and unembarrassed opportunity for the independent determination of her own political development and national policy and assure her of a sincere welcome into the society of free nations under institutions of her own choosing ...

'(7) Belgium, the whole world will agree, must be evacuated and restored, without any attempts to limit the sovereignty which she enjoys in common with all other free nations ...

'(11) Rumania, Serbia and Montenegro should be evacuated; *The Balkans* occupied territories restored; Serbia accorded free and secure access to the sea; and the relations of the several Balkans States to one another determined by friendly counsel along historically established lines of allegiance and nationality; and international guarantees of the political and economic independence and territorial integrity of the several Balkan states should be entered into.

'(12) The Turkish portions of the present Ottoman Empire should be assured a secure sovereignty, but the other nationalities which are now under Turkish rule should be assured an undoubted security of life and an absolutely unmolested opportunity of autonomous development . . . the Dardanelles should be permanently opened as a free passage to the ships and commerce of all nations under international guarantees.

'(13) An independent Polish state should be erected which *Poland* should include the territories inhabited by indisputably Polish populations, which should be assured a free and secure access to the sea, and whole political and economic independence and territorial integrity should be guaranteed by international covenant.

'(14) A general association of nations must be formed under *League of* specific covenants for the purpose of affording mutual guarantees *Nations* of political independence and territorial integrity to great and small states alike (1).'

1 Versailles 1919: Victory and Defeat

PEACE came as a surprise. Allied military experts had said a German collapse could not be expected before summer 1919. The peacemakers were therefore unprepared.

There were other more important complications, however. First, many people wanted to sign the treaty—a proliferation of nations, with conflicting aims, each insisting on having a say in the settlements. Many of these nations had entered into secret agreements among themselves before America entered the war and before President Wilson's 'Fourteen Points'. There was the confusion, too, created by these Points, some vague, some expressing American self-interest, some aimed at reassuring Russia of American intentions, some hopelessly idealistic. They were not accepted in their entirety by the Allies.

Many peacemakers

With the Armistice came the impassioned cry that *now* was the time to settle all differences. Delays were resented. What did the peacemakers want to do, and how were they to do it? The peacemaking machinery itself was cumbersome. The result was undue haste in some respects; important matters were overlooked or put aside—including the amount of reparations the Germans were to pay. The public as a whole believed the total should not be influenced by Germany's ability to find it. As *The Times* said: 'The only possible motive in determining their capacity to pay must be the interest of the Allies'; and *The Daily Mail*, on 15 December 1918, was even more outspoken: 'Germany can pay, if there is any ginger in the Allied Governments!'

Reparations

Against this noisy background, the peacemakers who flocked to Paris had two main tasks: to remove future threats from Germany

13

Opposite Woodrow Wilson, President of the United States (1913–21) whose idealistic views were not entirely accepted by the Allies

and satisfy the desires of the victors for revenge, and to reshape Europe. The methods used were the territorial changes and the harsh disarmament terms in the Treaty of Versailles (reproduced in extract at the end of this Chapter). Warnings by some statesmen against revenge were overlooked. Lloyd George told his Liberal supporters in a meeting at 10 Downing Street on 12 November:

'No settlement which contravenes the principles of eternal justice will be a permanent one. Let us be warned by the example of 1871. We must not allow any sense of revenge, any spirit of greed, any grasping desire, to over-ride the fundamental principle of righteousness. Vigorous attempts will be made to hector and bully the Government in an endeavour to make them depart from the strict principles of right and to satisfy some base, sordid, squalid ideas of vengeance and of avarice ... (2)'

But satisfying the wishes of the victors was a complicated business. The Allies disagreed among themselves. Attitudes towards the important question of the Rhineland are one example. The French, led by Clemenceau, wanted indefinite control as a guarantee of French security. The British and Americans could not agree to this permanent separation of the Rhineland from Germany.

Eventually, a compromise was reached, under which America and Britain guaranteed to support France immediately if she were ever attacked again by Germany—a guarantee which was to lapse through the American refusal to ratify the Treaty of Versailles. This gave Britain, too, the chance to claim freedom from her part of the bargain. It was a muddled affair.

The French began to feel that, to look after themselves, they must go it alone. Treaties were hurriedly signed with Poland, Yugoslavia, Czechoslovakia and Rumania. Confusion was made worse, for the fate of France in West Europe was now inextricably bound up with that of unstable nations in East Europe. Chances of France being dragged into war were increased—and with France, Britain. As in 1914, the world still faced the danger of a global conflict sparked off by a comparatively localized incident.

None of the major powers really felt happy about the Treaty. Germany was still the largest national block in Europe. As Marshal Foch said drily, 'This is not peace. It is an Armistice for twenty years.'

Left Lloyd George arrives at the Paris Peace conference in 1919. *Right* Clemenceau, the French premier

THE TREATY OF VERSAILLES, 28 JUNE 1919

'(42) Germany is forbidden to maintain or construct any forti- *Treaty of* fications either on the left bank of the Rhine or on the right bank to *Versailles* the west of a line drawn 50 kilometres to the east of the Rhine.

'(45) As compensation for the destruction of the coal-mines in *Reparations* the north of France, and as part payment towards the total reparation due from Germany for the damage resulting from the war, Germany cedes to France in full and absolute possession, with exclusive rights of exploitation, unencumbered and free from all debts and charges of any kind, the coal-mines situated in the Saar Basin ...

'(49) ... At the end of fifteen years from the coming into force of *German Empire* the present Treaty, the inhabitants of the said territory shall be *overthrown* called upon to indicate the sovereignty under which they desire to be placed.

'(80) Germany acknowledges and will respect strictly the independence of Austria, within the frontiers which may be fixed in a Treaty between that State and the Principal Allied and Associated Powers; she agrees that this independence shall be inalienable, except with the consent of the Council of the League of Nations.

'(87) Germany, in conformity with the action already taken by the Allied and Associated Powers, recognizes the complete independence of Poland, and renounces in her favour all rights and title over the territory [defined in detail] ...

'(88) In the portion of Upper Silesia included within the bound-

15

aries described below, the inhabitants will be called upon to indicate by a vote whether they wish to be attached to Germany or to Poland ...

'(116) [Germany accepts] the abrogation of the Brest–Litovsk Treaties ...

'(119) Germany renounces in favour of the Principal Allied and Associated Powers all her rights and titles over her oversea possessions ...

Army disbanded
'(160)(*i*) By a date which must not be later than March 31, 1920, the German Army must not comprise more than seven divisions of infantry and three divisions of cavalry. After that date the total number of effectives in the Army ... must not exceed one hundred thousand men, including officers and establishments of depots. The Army shall be devoted exclusively to the maintenance of order within the territory and to the control of the frontiers. The total effective strength of officers, including personnel of staffs ... must not exceed four thousand ...

'(*iii*) ... the Great German General Staff and all similar organizations shall be dissolved and may not be reconstituted in any form ...

'(173) Universal compulsory military service shall be abolished in Germany. The German Army may only be constituted and recruited by means of voluntary enlistment.

'(181) ... The German naval forces in commission must not exceed 6 battleships ..., 6 light cruisers, 12 destroyers, 12 torpedo boats, or an equal number of ships constructed to replace them ... No submarines are to be included ...

'(191) The construction or acquisition of any submarine, even for commercial purposes, shall be forbidden in Germany ...

'(198) The armed forces of Germany must not include any military or naval air forces ...

'(203) All the military, naval and air clauses contained in the present Treaty, for the execution of which a time-limit is prescribed, shall be executed by Germany under the control of Inter-Allied Commissions specially appointed for this purpose by the Principal Allied and Associated Powers.

'War guilt'
clauses
'(227) The Allied and Associated Powers publicly arraign William II of Hohenzollern, formerly German Emperor, for a

supreme offence against international morality and the sanctity of treaties.

'(231) The Allied and Associated Governments affirm and Germany accepts responsibility of Germany and her allies for causing the loss and damage to which the Allied and Associated Governments and their nationals have been subjected as a consequence of the war imposed upon them by the aggression of Germany and her allies.

'(232) The Allied and Associated Governments recognize that the resources of Germany are not adequate, after taking into account permanent diminutions of such resources which will result from other provisions of the present Treaty, to make complete reparation for all such loss and damage. The Allied and Associated Governments, however, require, and Germany undertakes, that she will make compensation for all damage done to the civilian population of the Allied and Associated Powers and to their property during the period of the belligerency of each ...

'(233) The amount of the above damage ... shall be determined by an Inter-Allied Commission, to be called the Reparation Commission [which shall] draw up a schedule of payments prescribing the time and manner for securing and discharging the entire obligation within a period of thirty years from May 1, 1921 ...

'(428) As a guarantee for the execution of the present Treaty by Germany, the German territory situated to the west of the Rhine, together with the bridgeheads, will be occupied by Allied and Associated troops for a period of fifteen years ...(3).'

Rhineland occupied

2 Old Wine in New Bottles

FOR A BRIEF time, with the recreation of political structures, the idea of democracy was taken up in Europe by all the new states and by all the defeated states. But true democratic traditions were lacking; law and order was weak or non-existent. National unity itself was fleeting, and there were conflicts of interest inside the new nations. Many faced the ebbing and flowing threat from Communism. *New democracies*

The German nation suffered defeat, starvation and chaos. What did the defeated German soldiers feel? Soldiers' Councils, influenced by Communism, were formed by thousands of men streaming back from the fighting, but they were opposed by military volunteer *Freikorps* groups. By the summer of 1919 there were 200,000 of these 'free troops', who themselves shouted extremist slogans and stirred up political unrest. *German bitterness*

It was left to the Social Democrats to build a new German Republic. It was a thankless task. Faced with the threat of civil war, the Government appealed for calm: 'We do not want the horrors of civil war, with its murderous battling of brother against brother ... to destroy our Fatherland.'

A National Assembly was elected in January 1919, and met at Weimar on 6 February to formulate the new constitution, published on 11 August. Fehrenbach, who was to become Chancellor in June 1920, cried: 'May it make the German people the most peace-loving in the world.' The Constitution was liberal, and introduced votes for all. But it contained a number of drawbacks. *A new constitution*

First, it introduced the parliamentary system of proportional representation, with a proliferation of parties. Second, it created the

Opposite According to General Ludendorff the German army had been sacrificed by her politicians

post of President of the Republic—to replace the Emperor—who was elected by the people for a seven year term, and who was to choose the Chancellor. Under Article 48, the President could have absolute power in an emergency with the Chancellor's assent. This power, if it fell into the wrong hands, could be disastrous. Let us look at how the constitution worked:

THE WEIMAR CONSTITUTION, 11 AUGUST 1919

'This constitution has been framed by the united German people, inspired by the determination to restore and establish their Federation upon a basis of liberty and justice, to be of service to the cause of peace both at home and abroad, and to promote social progress.

'(1) The German Federation is a republic ...

'(5) The executive power is exercised in Federal affairs through the institutions of the Federation in virtue of the Federal Constitution, and in State affairs by the officials of the State, in virtue of the Constitution of the States.

'(6) The Federal Government has the sole legislative power as regards: (*a*) Foreign relations; (*b*) Colonial affairs; (*c*) Nationality, right of domicile, immigration, emigration and extradition; (*d*) Military organisation; (*e*) The monetary system; (*f*) The customs departments, as well as uniformity of commercial intercourse; (*g*) The postal and telegraph services, including the telephone service.

'(7) The Federal Government has legislative powers as regards: (1) Civic rights; (2) Penal power; (3) Judicial procedure ... (6) The press, trade unions, and the rights of assembly ... (9) Labour laws ... (15) Traffic in foodstuffs and luxuries as well as in articles of daily necessity ... (20) Theatres and cinemas ...

'(13) Federal law overrides state law ...

'(20) The Reichstag is an assembly composed of the deputies of the German people.

'(21) The deputies are representatives of the whole people. They are subject to their conscience only, and not bound by any mandates.

'(22) The deputies are elected by the universal, equal, direct and secret suffrage of all men and women above the age of twenty, upon the principles of proportional representation ...

'(25) The President of the Federation may dissolve the Reichstag, but only once for any one reason. The general election will take place not later than sixty days after the dissolution ...

'(41) The President of the Federation is elected by the whole German people. Every German who has completed his thirty-fifth year is eligible ...

'(47) The President of the Federation has supreme command over all the armed forces of the Federation.

'(48) In the case of a State not fulfilling the duties imposed on it by the Federal Constitution or the Federal laws, the President of the Federation may enforce their fulfilment with the help of armed forces. *Emergency laws*

'Where public security and order are seriously disturbed or endangered within the Federation, the President of the Federation may take the measures necessary for their restoration, intervening in case of need with help of armed forces. For this purpose he is permitted, for the time being, to abrogate, either wholly or partially, the fundamental laws laid down in [these] articles.

'The President of the Federation must, without delay, inform the Reichstag of any measures taken in accordance with paragraphs one and two of this Article. Such measures shall be withdrawn upon the demand of the Reichstag.

'Where there is danger in delay, the State Government may take provisional measures of the kind described in paragraph 2 for its own territory. Such measures shall be withdrawn upon the demand of the President of the Federation or the Reichstag ...

'(52) The Federal Government consists of the Chancellor of the Federation and the Federal Ministers. *The Chancellor*

'(53) The President ... appoints and dismisses the Chancellor ... and, on the latter's recommendations, the ... Ministers.

'(54) The Chancellor [and the] Ministers require, for the administration of their office, the confidence of the Reichstag. Any one of them must resign, should the confidence of the House be withdrawn by an express resolution.

'(56) The Chancellor ... determines the main lines of policy, for which he is responsible to the Reichstag ...(4)'

This then, was the Weimar Constitution, with which Germany was to face the future.

The National Assembly now set up an inquiry into the causes of

21

'Stab in the back' Germany's defeat. The 'stab in the back' legend grew up at this time, for according to Hindenburg—under pressure from Ludendorff—the German Army had been stabbed in the back by the German politicians. Or so he had been told by a British general. This legend poisoned the well-meaning atmosphere of the new Weimar Republic from the very start. In any case, the Republic was regarded by many as a burden imposed by the Allies.

Demobilized soldiers grew even more bitter and restless. Officers pointed out that the last battle of the war had never been fought. It had been the politicians who had signed surrender, not them. Hindenburg, who had not attended the signing of the armistice, continued as Chief of the General Staff.

Hitler was later to make use of the 'stab in the back' legend, branding the politicians who had made the peace in November 1918 as the 'November criminals'.

War guilt Attitudes in Germany were already hardening over the war guilt clause in Article 231 of the Versailles Treaty. This clause was itself based on the Report of the Commission on the Responsibility of the Authors of the War, which stated:

'The War was premeditated by the Central Powers together with their allies, Turkey and Bulgaria, and was the result of acts deliberately committed in order to make it unavoidable. Germany, in agreement with Austria–Hungary, deliberately worked to defeat all the many conciliatory proposals made by the Entente Powers.'

German nationalism Many Germans loudly disagreed. Coupled with the stab in the back theory, this made chances of unity in the country even more slight. Nationalist feelings were rekindled, fired by fears of the Communist threat and Communist terrorism, such as the rising led by Max Hölz in Prussia in March 1921. His placards proclaimed: 'DICTATORSHIP OF THE PROLETARIAT! We have occupied the area with our Red troops and hereby proclaim proletarian martial law, to the effect that EVERY INHABITANT WILL BE SHOT who does not comply with the ordinances of the Military Command. The moment reports reach us that the Security Police or the Army are approaching, we will at once SET FIRE TO THE ENTIRE CITY AND SLAUGHTER THE BOURGEOSIE without distinction as to sex or age'.

Austria–Hungary Austria–Hungary emerged from the war unrecognizable. New nations were hacked out of the remains of the old Austro–Hungarian

Thomas Masaryk was first president of the new state,
Czechoslovakia, created from the ruins of the old Austria–Hungary

Empire under the Treaty of St Germain, modelled on the Treaty of Versailles.

The new states of Czechoslovakia and Yugoslavia were set up. Austria had to give further territory to Italy. *Anschluss*, union of Austria with Germany, was clearly forbidden.

But Yugoslavia, Czechoslovakia and Rumania—created from the Hungarian territory of Transylvania—shared a common fear, as indeed they might—the rebirth of Austro–Hungarian efforts to build an Empire. In 1921, therefore, the three countries signed a treaty to protect the new *status quo*. Ominously, this treaty came to be called 'The Little Entente'. (It was alleged fear of the Anglo–French Entente which had played a major part in Austro–German actions in 1914.)

Balkans: 'Little Entente'

Meanwhile, these vulnerable new nations were beset by problems. Democracy was striven for, but it was a difficult task. Czechoslovakia faced the added problem of having three million German-speaking citizens in the country, many of them fervent Pan-Germans who despised the Czechs. Later the name of these Sudeten Germans was to become news.

At first however, Czechoslovakia made a good start. She was

23

Danzig, nominally a Free City, was claimed both by the Poles and the Germans

lucky in her first President, Thomas Masaryk, who believed 'Democracy is the rule of the people, but there can be no government without obedience and discipline.'

Poland What of Poland? The Allies made up their minds to recreate the state of Poland, despite the fact it had been swallowed up by its neighbours more than a hundred years before the First World War began. It was a tricky decision. Resurrecting Poland brought problems of territorial boundaries and conflicting national feelings, leading, for example, to the conflict over Teschen, which was eventually given to the Czechs in July 1920, much to the anger of the Poles—and which was to be taken back again during the rape of Czechoslovakia by Adolf Hitler nearly twenty years later.

Danzig: a free Poland was dangerously poised between the powers of Russia
city in the East and Germany in the West, each with territorial claims on the new country. Chief among the German–Polish disputes was the port of Danzig at the mouth of the Vistula. Who should have it? The river was the most important in Poland, yet the town had mainly a German population.

 In the end, Danzig was made into a Free City. But the quarrel

Left Korfanty and *right* Pilduski, two men who tried to strengthen Poland by seizing territory on her borders

continued to be a bone of discontent.

So did the question of Upper Silesia. Korfanty attempted to seize the area for Poland in August 1919 but was resisted by German volunteers. Early in 1920, allied troops occupied the territory, but the result of a plebiscite held in March 1921 was such a narrow victory for Poland that the League of Nations decided the country must be divided.

On the eastern front, Poland's Marshal Pilduski decided to *Treaty of Riga* exploit Russia's internal disorders and march with Polish troops into the Ukraine in 1920. Kiev was occupied on 7 May, the aim being to set up a Polish–Ukrainian 'Federation'. A Russian counter-attack reached Warsaw in August but the Russian troops were then defeated. The Communists had no choice but to sign the Treaty of Riga in March 1921. About six million Orthodox Ukrainians and White Russians were brought, largely against their will, into Poland. The peace seemed a strange one to them.

When the Armistice was signed, Russia was already submerged in *Russian* problems of her own. In autumn 1917 the Bolsheviks had seized *Revolution* power from the provisional liberal Government which had over- *(1917)*

thrown the Tzar six months before. The victory of the revolution was proclaimed at the end of October:

'To the Citizens of Russia! The Provisional Government has been deposed. State power has passed into the hands of the organ of the Petrograd Soviet of Workers' and Soldiers' Deputies—the Revolutionary Military Commitee, which heads the Petrograd proletariat and garrison. The cause for which the people have fought, namely, the immediate offer of a democratic peace, the abolition of landlord ownership, workers' control over production, and the establishment of Soviet Power—this cause has been secured. Long live the revolution of workers, soldiers and peasants!'

Russian 'Decree on Peace'

It was clear to the Council of Commissars, headed by Lenin and with Trotsky in charge of defence and foreign affairs, that Russia must sue for peace with Germany as soon as possible. On 26 October 1917, a 'Decree on Peace' was issued. Here are its main points:

'The Workers' and Peasants' Government ... proposes to all warring peoples and their Governments that negotiations leading to a just peace begin at once.

'The just and democratic peace for which the great majority of war-exhausted, tormented toilers and labouring classes of all belli-

Demonstrators during the Russian Revolution seen outside the Winter Palace, Petrograd, in 1917

gerent countries are thirsting; the peace for which the Russian workers and peasants are so insistently and loudly clamouring since the overthrow of the Tzarist regime is, in the opinion of the Government, an immediate peace without annexation (i.e. without the seizure of foreign lands and the forcible taking over of other nationalities) and without indemnity.

'The Russian Government proposes that this kind of peace be concluded immediately between all the warring nations. It offers to take decisive steps at once, without the least delay, without waiting for a final confirmation of all the terms of such a peace by conferences of popular representatives of all countries and all nations ...

'To prolong this war because the rich and strong nations cannot agree how to divide the small and weak nationalities which they have seized is, in the opinion of the Government, a most criminal act against humanity, and it solemnly announces its decision to sign at once terms of peace bringing this war to an end on the indicated conditions ...

'Moreover, the Government declares that it does not regard the above mentioned terms of peace in the light of an ultimatum. It will agree to examine all other terms. It will insist only that whatever

More demonstrations in Petrograd; on the banners are pictures and inscriptions of the revolutionaries

belligerent nation has anything to propose, it should do so quickly, in the clearest terms, leaving out all double meanings and all secrets in making the proposal ...(5)'

Treaty of Brest-Litovsk
Very soon after, in March 1918, the Russians signed the humiliating Treaty of Brest–Litovsk with Germany. It was a humiliation indeed, as can be seen from its main terms:

'(1) The Central Powers and Russia declare the state of war between them to be terminated and are resolved henceforth to live in peace and friendship with one another ...

A smaller Russia
'(3) The regions lying west of the line agreed upon by the contracting parties and formerly belonging to Russia, shall no longer be under Russian Sovereignty. It is agreed that the line appears from the appended map, No. 1, which, as agreed upon, forms an essential part of the peace treaty [Finland, the Baltic States, Poland, and the Ukraine were to be detached from Russia]. The regions in question will have no obligation whatever toward Russia, arising from their former relations thereto. Russia undertakes to refrain from all interference in the internal affairs of these territories and to let Germany and Austria determine the future fate of these territories in agreement with their populations.

'(4) Germany and Austria agree, when a general peace is concluded and Russian demobilization is fully completed to evacuate the regions east of the line designated in Article 3 ... Russia will do everything in her power to complete as soon as possible the evacuation of the Anatolian provinces and their orderly return to Turkey. The districts of Erivan, Kars and Batum will likewise without delay be evacuated by Russian troops. Russia will not interfere in the reorganization of the constitutional or international conditions of these districts, but leaves it to the populations of the districts to carry out the reorganization ...

Russian demobil- ization
'(5) Russia will without delay carry out the complete demobilization of her army, including the forces newly formed by the present Government. Russia will further transfer her warships to Russian harbours and leave them there until a general peace or immediately disarm ...

'(9) The contracting parties mutually renounce indemnification of ... war costs ... as well as indemnification for war damages ... (6)'

Opposite top Trotsky inspects a regiment of the Red Army; *below* Lenin addresses a meeting (November, 1917)

Russia now withdrew from European affairs and fought her civil war for the next three years. By the summer of 1920 the most serious threat to the Bolsheviks came from Poland, supported by the French; and in 1920 came the Polish invasion and the defeat outside Warsaw. The Soviet leaders were demoralized and still had to deal with the exhaustion and starvation of millions of fellow-Russians.

Kronstadt Mutiny   In March 1921 came a mutiny of sailors at Kronstadt. Their demands were a serious threat to Lenin's plans:

'Having heard the report of the representatives of the Crews, despatched by the General Meeting of the Crews from the ships to Petrograd in order to learn the state of affairs in Petrograd we decided:

'(1) In view of the fact that the present Soviets do not represent the will of the workers and peasants, immediately to re-elect the Soviets by secret voting, with free preliminary agitation among all workers and peasants before the elections.

'(2) Freedom of speech, and press for workers, peasants, Anarchists and Left Socialist Parties.

'(3) Freedom of meetings, trade unions and peasant associations.

'(4) To convene … a nonparty conference of workers, soldiers and sailors of Petrograd City, Kronstadt and Petrograd Province.

'(5) To liberate all political prisoners of Socialist Parties, and also all workers, peasants, soldiers and sailors who have been imprisoned in connexion with working class and peasant movements.

'(6) To elect a commission to review the cases of those who are imprisoned in gaols and concentration camps.

'(7) To abolish all Political Departments, because no single party may enjoy privileges in the propaganda of its ideas and receive funds from the state for this purpose (7).'

Lenin ruthlessly put the mutiny down, but he saw that he would have to revise his previous ideas on communism, and make a partial return to individual ownership.

He explained in 1921: 'The peculiarity of war communism consisted in the fact that we really took from the peasants all their surpluses, and sometimes even what was not surplus but part of what was necessary to feed the peasant, we took it to cover the costs of the army and to maintain the workers.'

Death of Lenin   This harsh policy, he now realised, would have to be altered. But

Two bitter enemies, *left* Stalin, who became Secretary of the Communist Party after Lenin's death and *right* Mussolini, founder of the Italian Fascist Party. In 1923, four years after he had founded the Fascists, Mussolini became Prime Minister of Italy.

in May 1922, Lenin suffered his first heart attack, followed by another in the autumn. Stalin, Trotsky's bitter enemy and now powerful Communist Party Secretary, began to gain even more control. Early in 1924, Lenin died, mourned by millions. The Stalin–Trotsky battle for power raged.

In Italy, meanwhile, there were demands for workers' councils, *Italy* excited by the promises of Communism. In opposition, anti-Communist war veterans began to form military groups. Benito Mussolini, a leftist journalist, founded his so-called Fascist Party in March 1919.

The Communist threat continued, and by 1921 the Socialists were *Mussolini* divided and weakened. The Italian leader, Giolitti, proposed an *marches on* alliance with the Fascists, hoping to use them to strengthen his *Rome* position, and thirty-five Fascist deputies were brought into the *(1922)* Parliament. Mussolini prepared a *coup* and marched on Rome in October 1922.

'Fascisti! Italians!' he proclaimed in his manifesto (26 October),

31

Autumn 1935, a Young Fascist march-past before Mussolini

Fascist Manifesto

'The time for determined battle has come! Four years ago the National Army loosed at this season the final offensive, which brought it to victory. Today the army of the Black-shirts takes again possession of that victory, which has been mutilated, and going directly to Rome brings victory again to the glory of that capital. From now on principi and triari are mobilized. The martial law of Fascism now becomes a fact. By order of the Duce all the military, political, and administrative functions of the party management are taken over by a secret Quadrumvirate of Action with dictatorial powers.

'The Army, the reserve and safeguard of the Nation, must not take part in this struggle. Fascism renews its highest homage given to the Army of Vittorio Veneto. Fascism, furthermore, does not march against the police, but against a political class both cowardly and imbecile, which in four long years has not been able to give a

Government to the nation. Those who form the productive class must know that Fascism wants to impose nothing more than order and discipline upon the nation and to help to raise the strength which will renew progress and prosperity ...

'Fascism draws its sword to cut the multiple Gordian knots which tie and burden Italian life. We call God and the spirit of our five hundred thousand dead to witness that only one impulse sends us on, that only one passion burns within us—the impulse and the passion to contribute to the safety and greatness of our country.

'Fascisti of all Italy! Stretch forth like Romans your spirits and your fibres! We must win! We will.

'Long live Italy! Long live Fascism! (8)'

Mussolini's armed men found little resistance, and on 30 October the king invited Mussolini to become Prime Minister. Mussolini was arriving. He gained additional popular support in July 1923, sending in troops to annex the free city of Fiume, and still more in August when he seized Corfu after the Italian General Tellini had been murdered in Greece. (Tellini had been President of the International Commission for the delimitation of the Greco–Albanian border.) *Mussolini as Prime Minister*

Meanwhile, in Germany, the Nazi movement saw Mussolini as an example of how a small group of men could seize power. Hermann Esser told a meeting in Munich on 3 November 1922: 'What a handful of brave men can do in Italy is not beyond us. In Bavaria we too have a Mussolini. His name is Adolf Hitler!' *'Il Duce'*

In December 1925, two important laws were passed in Italy which increased Mussolini's power and freed him still more from the restrictions of Parliamentary Government. He now became a political dictator. These were the laws:

ITALIAN LAW ON THE POWERS AND PREROGATIVES OF THE HEAD OF THE GOVERNMENT, 24 DECEMBER 1925 *Fascist laws*

'(1) The executive power is exercised by His Majesty the King through his Government. The Government consists of the Prime Minister, Secretary of State and the Ministers Secretaries of State. The Prime Minister is Head of the Government.

'(2) The Head of the Government ... is appointed and recalled by the King and is responsible to the King for the general policy of the Government ...

33

'(3) The Head of the Government ... directs and co-ordinates the activities of the Ministers, settles disputes among them, calls meetings of the Council of Ministers and presides over them ...

'(6) No bill or motion may be submitted to either of the Houses of Parliament without the consent of the Head of the Government.

'The Head of the Government has the power to request that a bill, rejected by one of the Houses of Parliament, be voted upon again three months after the first vote. In such cases the vote is by ballot without previous debate ...

'The Head of the Government also has the power to request that a bill rejected by one of the Houses be submitted to the other House to be voted upon after due examination ...(9)'

More Fascist   ITALIAN LAW ON THE POWER OF THE EXECUTIVE BRANCH TO MAKE
legislation   DECREES HAVING THE FORCE OF LAWS, 31 JANUARY 1926

'(1) By Royal Decree, after deliberation in the Council of Ministers and hearing in the Council of State, regulations having the force of Laws may be issued concerning the following, even in matters heretofore regulated by law:

(*a*) The execution of laws.

(*b*) The use of powers belonging to the executive branch.

(*c*) The organization and functioning of the State administrations and of their personnel; the organization of public institutions and concerns ...

'Expenditures provided for by a Finance Act must continue to be authorized by an Act of Parliament ...

'(3) By Royal Decree, after deliberation in the Council of Ministers, regulations having the force of laws may be issued in the following cases:

(*a*) When the Government is empowered and delegated to do so by a law ...

(*b*) When the case is exceptional by reason of its urgency or absolute necessity; whether or not a case is exceptional shall be judged only by Parliament.

'In cases referred to in Paragraph (2) ... The Royal Decree shall contain a clause providing for presentation to Parliament for ratification; the Decree ceases to have effect unless it is submitted to one of the Houses of Parliament for ratification, and this should be done not later than at the third session after the publication of the

Decree ...(10)'

The League of Nations was founded after the Armistice. In fact the Covenant of the League was used as the opening statement of the Treaty of Versailles. The League was linked with the Treaty, and each had to suffer the weaknesses of the other. Both were framed in the hope there would be lasting peace between nations. *League of Nations*

COVENANT OF THE LEAGUE OF NATIONS 28 JUNE 1919 *Covenant of the League*

The High Contracting Parties

'In order to promote international co-operation and to achieve international peace and security,

'By the acceptance of obligations not to resort to war,

'By the prescription of open, just and honourable relations between nations,

'By the firm establishment of the understanding of international law as the actual rule of conduct among Governments, and

'By the maintenance of justice and a scrupulous respect for all treaty obligations in the dealings of organized peoples with one another,

'*Agree* to this Covenant of the League of Nations ...

The first session of the League of Nations in 1920

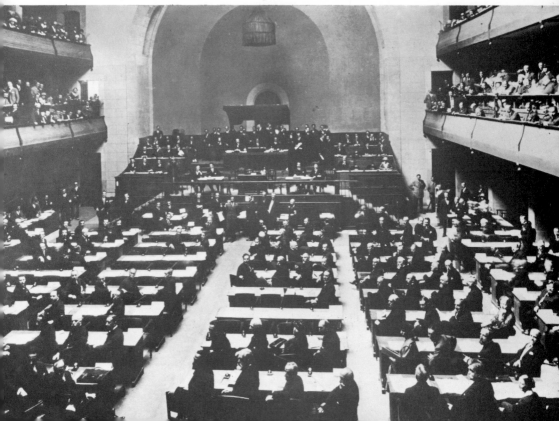

'(5) Except where otherwise expressly provided in this Covenant or by the terms of the present Treaty, decisions at any meeting of the Assembly or of the Council shall require the agreement of all the Members of the League represented at the meeting.

'(8) The Members of the League recognize that the maintenance of peace requires the reduction of national armaments to the lowest point consistent with national safety and the enforcement by common action of international obligations ... The Members of the League undertake to interchange full and frank information as to the scale of their armaments.

'(10) The Members of the League undertake to respect and preserve as against external aggression the territorial integrity and existing political independence of all Members of the League.

'(13) The Members of the League agree that whenever any dispute shall arise between them which they recognize to be suitable for submission to arbitration and which cannot be satisfactorily settled by diplomacy, they will submit the whole subject-matter to arbitration.

'(16) Should any Member of the League resort to war in disregard of its Covenants under Articles 12, 13 or 15, it shall *ipso facto* be deemed to have committed an act of war against all other Members of the League, which hereby undertake immediately to subject it to the severance of all trade or financial relations, the prohibition of all intercourse between their nationals and the nationals of the Covenant-breaking State, and the prevention of all financial, commercial and personal intercourse between the nationals of the Covenant-breaking State and the nationals of any other State, whether a Member of the League or not (11).'

Such was the Covenant of the ill-fated League of Nations. High international hopes for the League were doomed to failure, but the League did have some value as an international forum. It was also a way of dealing with minority complaints from citizens in the new nations which had appeared on the map of Europe.

The League was primarily a multilateral treaty. Each member promised to seek peaceful solutions to disputes, and to share the defence of each other. This was the principle of 'collective security' as stated in Article 10 of the Covenant.

But obligations lacked clarity. An effort to strengthen the

machinery through the Geneva Protocol of October 1924 failed, largely because Britain believed its stress on automatic sanctions was too strong.

Geneva Protocol

The League of Nations was not a government, with governmental powers. Apart from anything else, it lacked armies to back up its policies. It could only keep the peace if its members wanted peace. Early after the war, most people felt the members did want an end to wars, and that the rulers who had led countries to war in 1914 had been overthrown in favour of democracies.

Limitations of League

President Wilson told the Paris Conference on 25 January 1919:

'Gentlemen, the select classes of mankind are no longer the governors of mankind. The fortunes of mankind are now in the hands of the plain people of the whole world ... We are here to see, in short, that the very foundations of this war are swept away.'

He added, 'Those foundations were the private choice of small countries of civil rulers and military staffs. Those foundations were the aggression of great powers upon small. Those foundations were the holding together of Empires of unwilling subjects by the duress of arms. Those foundations were the power of small bodies of men to work their will and use mankind as pawns in a game.'

But the League failed in its task of collective security. America herself did not become a member, and Germany and Russia were at first kept out. This left Britain, France and Italy as the major power members. Yet Italy successfully defied the League by bombarding the Island of Corfu in 1923. Also in 1923, France occupied the Ruhr, an action which Britain opposed. So much for collective security.

Non-members

The machinery of the League was inadequate. It lacked teeth. In theory, every member in the Assembly had a vote, but on all important issues voting had to be unanimous for action to be taken. Consequently, nothing was ever done.

As if this were not enough, there was the basic difference of attitude by Britain and France towards Germany and, linked with this, towards the question of disarmament. Invaded twice in fifty years, France had a deep fear of Germany; Britain ignored the threat even when it appeared. Britain maintained disarmament was a source of security. France believed security had to come before disarmament. The difference was fundamental.

Britain and France

3 Reparations

DEFEAT had disastrous results on German finances. The German leaders had borrowed heavily during the war, believing victory would cover the cost. Then, when it was all over, most of the allied nations pressed for huge reparations, based on a false hope that the destruction of war can be paid for.

Compensation for war damage

The allied Note of 5 November 1918 specified: 'Compensation will be made by Germany for all the damage done to the civilian populations of the Allies and their property.' This was included in the Versailles Treaty as Article 232, immediately after the Article containing the 'war guilt' clause. Both were the source of long grievance among the German people.

The reparation issue became a bitter source of controversy for another reason. No exact reparation sum was agreed by the Allies before the Treaty was signed, because they were in such a hurry to conclude it. Germany had to sign a blank cheque until the sum could be agreed.

A blank cheque

Article 233 required Germany to be told of the amount not later than 1 May 1921. In Paris, January 1921, the bill was added up. Germany was to pay two series of forty-two annuities, one being fixed at six million gold marks in 1923 and remaining at this level until 1963, the other amounting to twelve per cent of the annual value of German exports.

The Germans said the demands were far too high for a defeated nation to meet. Marshal Foch replied by sending in French troops to occupy Duisberg, Düsseldorf and Ruhrort. German militants reacted strongly. On 26 August Erzeberger, who had signed the Armistice in November 1918, was murdered. Rathenau, a Jew who

French occupy Ruhr

39

Opposite An early photograph of Hitler in September 1923, just before the failure of the Munich putsch

Defeat angered many Germans, and Erzeberger (*left*) and Rathenau (*right*) were both murdered for their part in accepting it

as Foreign Minister had agreed to the Treaty of Rapallo, was also murdered in June 1922.

Allies disagree   A further complication to the reparation question was that, not only were there disagreements between the Allies and Germany, but also between the Allies themselves. Britain, with only minor land damage from the war, had a different attitude to that of France and Belgium, who had suffered great devastation. France also saw reparation as a means of keeping Germany weak.

'Balfour Note'   On 1 August 1922, in the 'Balfour Note' sent round to the Allied Governments, Britain said: '... in no circumstances do we propose to ask more from our debtors than is necessary to pay our creditors.' This was aimed at persuading the Americans to adopt an easier attitude towards British war debts. But it widened the rift between Britain and France.

Inflation of the mark   Inflation spread in Germany. By the end of 1922 the mark had dropped in value so much that the German Government could claim it was indeed impossible to make further payments. German workers were taking the worthless notes home in barrow-loads on pay day. But in January 1923, the Reparations Commission declared Germany was in default over her coal payments to the Allies. Britain abstained from this conclusion, but as a result of the Commission's findings, French and Belgian troops invaded the Ruhr, a key industrial region of Germany.

The German Government called upon industrialists and workers to resist passively: 'The action of the French and Belgian Governments in the Ruhr area constitutes a gross violation of international law and of the Treaty of Versailles. As a consequence all orders and ordinances directed to German officials in the course of this action are legally invalid. The Governments of the Reich, of Prussia, Bavaria, Hesse and Oldenburg therefore direct [all officials] not to obey the ordinances of the occupation Powers but only the ordinances of their own Governments ...(12)'

At the same time the German Government recklessly printed more and more paper money and the inflation became absurd. The mark collapsed, falling in value from 20,000 to the dollar in January 1923, to 100,000 in June, five million in August, 50 million by September, and 630,000 million in November. Many ordinary German people gave up money, and bartered for goods instead.

Hitler made his fiery attack—not on the French and Belgian troops—but on the Berlin Government and the Jews who had helped bring the Ruhr invasion about. He shouted at a Munich meeting: 'Not down with France, but down with the betrayers of the Fatherland. Down with the November criminals!' *Hitler and 'November criminals'*

President Ebert named Gustav Stresemann Chancellor on 13 August 1923. In an effort to restore economic life, Stresemann called off resistance on 26 September. His proclamation declared: *Stresemann's Proclamation*

'On 11 January French and Belgian troops occupied ... the German Ruhr territory. Since then, the Ruhr Territory and the Rhineland had to suffer severe oppression. Over 180,000 German men, women, old people and children have been driven from house and home. Millions of Germans no longer know what personal freedom is. Countless acts of violence have accompanied the occupation, more than one hundred fellow Germans lost their lives, hundreds are still languishing in prison.'

The Proclamation went on, 'A spirit of justice and of patriotism rose against the unlawfulness of the invasion. The population refused to work under foreign bayonets. For this loyalty and constancy ... the whole German people gives them thanks.

'The Reich Government undertook to do what it could for the suffering compatriots. An ever increasing amount of the means of the Reich has been claimed by this task. In the past week support for the Ruhr and the Rhineland amounted to 3,500 billion marks. In the current week a doubling of this sum is expected. Economic life in Germany, occupied or unoccupied, is disrupted. Perseverance in our present course threatens the terribly serious danger that it will be impossible to establish a stable currency, to maintain economic activity, and thus even to secure a bare existence for our people.'

Stresemann concluded, 'In the interest of Germany's future as well as in the interest of the Rhineland and the Ruhr the danger must be averted. To save the life of the people and of the State we face today the bitter necessity of breaking off the struggle ...(13)'

Nazi Party   But the catastrophic situation had made people flock to Hitler. His policy, laid down in the programme of his 'National Sozialistische Deutsche Arbeiter Partei' in February 1920, attracted more and more people:

'(1) We demand the union of all Germans in one Great Germany by the right of self-determination of peoples;

'(2) We demand the equality of the German nation with all other nations and abrogation of the Treaties of Versailles and St. Germain.

'(3) We demand land and territory for the feeding of our people and for the settlement of our surplus population.

'(4) Only those who are members of the nation can be citizens. Only those who are of German blood, without regard to religion, can be members of the German nation. No Jew can, therefore, be a member of the nation.

'(5) He who is not a citizen shall be able to live in Germany only as a guest and must live under laws governing foreigners ...(14)'

Hitler's   Stresemann read these reports anxiously. By November 1923 *putsch* Hitler believed he was strong enough to seize power in Munich. He *(1923)* persuaded Ludendorff to help him, and they believed the Bavarian Government would give support. But the Bavarian police struck back and Hitler was thrown into jail.

During his trial, held in Munich from 26 February to 1 April 1924, Hitler declared the *putsch* '... was to have the most tremendous effects on the domestic political scene. A type of Government which for five years has illegally been driving Germany towards death ... was to be smashed. In place of the internationally aided, Marxist, defeatist, pacifist, democratically orientated type of Government, there was to be established a nationalist Government ... All the proceedings had the purpose of affecting this upheaval (15).'

However, the present had to be faced. Hitler was sentenced to five years in Landsberg prison—though the sentence was soon reduced to thirteen months. Here he began to write the first draft of *Mein Kampf*—'My Struggle'—which later sold millions of copies throughout the world.

In Britain, the Government had persuaded America to take part in a full-scale inquiry into reparations. The outcome was the 1924 Dawes Plan, following the appointment of two committees of experts in November 1923: 'One will be charged with seeking methods of balancing the [German] budget and the measures to be taken to stabilize the currency. The other will have to seek the methods of estimating the amount of exported capital and of bringing it back into Germany.' *Reparations: the Dawes Plan*

The aim was to see just how Germany could pay up, without producing chaos all round. The Dawes Plan, accepted in 1924, proposed a two-year moratorium on payments, the return of the Ruhr to Germany, and a foreign loan to Germany of 80 million marks.

The Dawes Plan went into operation on 1 September. Germany and Europe were about to enjoy an interlude of five precious years of prosperity. This was how it was to be done:

THE DAWES PLAN, 1924 *Basis of Dawes plan*

I Attitude of the Committee

'(*a*) The standpoint adopted has been that of business and not politics.

'(*b*) Political factors have been considered only in so far as they affect the practicability of the plan.

'(*c*) The recovery of debt, not the imposition of penalties, has been sought.

'(*d*) The payment of that debt by Germany is her necessary contribution to repairing the damage of the war.

'(*e*) It is in the interest of all parties to carry out this plan in that good faith which is the fundamental of all business. Our plan is based upon this principle.

43

'(*f*) The reconstruction of Germany is not an end in itself; it is only part of the larger problem of the reconstruction of Europe.

'(*g*) Guarantees proposed are economic, not political.

Sanctions   III *Military Aspects—Contingent Sanctions and Guarantees*

'(*a*) Political guarantees and penalties are outside our jurisdiction.

'(*b*) The military aspect of this problem is beyond our terms of reference.

'(*c*) Within the unified territory, the plan requires that, when it is in effective operation:

'(1) if any military organization exists, it must not impede the free exercise of economic activities.   . .

'(2) there shall be no foreign economic control or interference other than that proposed by the plan.

'(*d*) But adequate and productive guarantees are provided.

Committee's   IV *The Committee's Task*
task

'(*a*) Stabilization of currency and the balancing of budgets are interdependent, though they are provisionally separable for examination.

'(*b*) Currency stability can only be maintained if the budget is normally balanced; the budget can only be balanced if a stable and reliable currency exists.

'(*c*) Both are needed to enable Germany to meet her internal requirements and Treaty payments.

Germany's   V *Economic Future of Germany*
economic
future   '(*a*) Productivity is expected from increasing population, technical skill, material resources and eminence in industrial science.

'(*b*) Plant capacity has been increased and improved since the war …(16)'

But while the Allies were thinking of economics, Germany was already turning her thoughts to armies.

Germany   Germany began to re-arm almost as soon as she was disarmed.
begins to   All possible use was made of the little she had been allowed to keep.
re-arm   Instead of the Great General Staff of 34,000 men, the Versailles Treaty only permitted the Operational General Staff—the *Truppengeneralstab*—of 4,000. General Hans von Seeckt, head of this stub of German military organisation, immediately set about finding ways in which it could be expanded when the time was ripe. The

same applied to the 100,000 troops allowed under the disarmament clauses. Von Seeckt saw them not as rankers, but as 100,000 leaders.

Seeckt also opened talks with Russia in early 1921 to find ways of getting round the Treaty. It was agreed Germans should join in tank and aircraft training on Russian soil. In 1922 the Treaty of Rapallo was signed between the two countries to put diplomatic and commercial relations on a normal footing. *Talks with Russia*

THE TREATY OF RAPALLO, 16 APRIL 1922 *Treaty of Rapallo*

'(1) The two Governments agree that the settlement ... of questions arising from the time when a state of war existed between Germany and Russia shall be effected on the following basis:

'(*a*) [The Parties] renounce mutually all compensation in respect of the costs of the war and of war losses ... also ... all compensation in respect of civilian losses caused ... by the so-called exceptional war legislation or by compulsory measures taken by State Departments of the other side.

'(*b*) The public and private legal relations between the two States ... will be settled on a basis of reciprocity.

'(*c*) Germany and Russia mutually renounce all compensation in respect of costs incurred on both sides for prisoners of war ...

'(3) Diplomatic and Consular relations will immediately be resumed ...

'(5) Both Governments will endeavour reciprocally to meet the economic needs of the other side in an accommodating spirit ...(17)'

Russia and Germany had much in common. Both could discuss their dislike of the new Poland. And with the alliance, Germany's diplomatic status was raised. The two outcasts of Europe were drawn closer together.

Meanwhile the Germans forged their new weapon, and disarmament clauses were quietly violated. Things were made easier for Germany after the Treaty of Locarno, when Britain and France decided to withdraw the Inter-Allied Control Commission in January 1927. The German Civil Air Transport now became the nucleus of a secret force of war planes; naval units were hidden in civil ministries; U-boats were illicitly built; new factories, many of them built with British and American re-construction loans, were designed so that they could be quickly turned over to war production. *German war plans*

4 Interlude: 1924-29

ALTHOUGH Gustav Stresemann was defeated in the Reichstag in November 1923, and lost the Chancellorship, he carried on as Foreign Minister until he died in October 1929. He wanted to serve German nationalism through subtle diplomacy rather than with an aggressive foreign policy. He even managed to work successfully with Aristide Briand, Foreign Minister of France. *Stresemann policy*

Stresemann believed Germany ought to join the League of Nations, and Germany applied for membership on 24 September 1924. Although Stresemann, as a good German, believed the post-war cession of land to Poland was intolerable, he realized the western frontier of Germany should be looked at before he tried to revise the eastern. So he proposed a joint guarantee of the Franco–German frontier by Germany, France, Britain and Italy.

Meantime, the domestic situation in Germany suffered another upheaval. Ebert, the first President, died in February 1925, and Hindenburg was elected to fill the post, much to Stresemann's dismay. The new President was old-fashioned, steeped in the Bismarckian traditions, and liable to become a figurehead for those who wanted Germany to have a mighty army once more. *President Hindenberg*

On 4 October 1925, representatives of Britain, France, Germany, Belgium and Italy met at Locarno to discuss the German frontier-guarantee proposals. On 16 October a series of treaties was signed, including the Treaty of Mutual Guarantee, the so-called Rhineland Pact. Here are its main points: *Locarno Pact*

'(1) The High Contracting Parties collectively and severally guarantee, in the manner provided in the following articles, the maintenance of the territorial status quo resulting from the frontiers

47

Opposite above Ramsay Macdonald and Briand the French Foreign Minister. *Below* Hindenburg, elected President of Germany in 1925

between Germany and Belgium and between Germany and France and the inviolability of the said frontiers [fixed by] the Treaty of Peace signed at Versailles on the 28 June 1919, and also the observance of the stipulations of Articles 42 and 43 of the said treaty concerning the demilitarized zone.

'(2) Germany and Belgium, and also Germany and France, mutually undertake that they will in no case attack or invade each other or resort to war against each other ...(18)'

France is over-committed The Locarno Treaties saddled France with far too many commitments. She undertook to guarantee the Czech and Polish frontiers, while Germany undertook to submit to arbitration any dispute arising over these frontiers. France, without partnership with Britain (who refused to become further involved) was becoming entangled. This is clearly seen from these extracts:

TREATY BETWEEN FRANCE AND CZECHOSLOVAKIA, 16 OCTOBER 1925

'(1) In the event of Czechoslovakia or France suffering from a failure to observe the undertakings arrived at this day between them and Germany with a view to the maintenance of general peace, France, and reciprocally Czechoslovakia, acting in application of Article 16 of the Covenant of the League of Nations, undertake to lend each other immediately aid and assistance, if such a failure is accompanied by an unprovoked recourse to arms.

'In the event of the Council of the League of Nations, when dealing with a question brought before it in accordance with the said undertakings, being unable to succeed in making its report accepted by all its members other than the representatives of the parties to the dispute, and in the event of Czechoslovakia or France being attacked with provocation, France, or reciprocally Czechoslovakia, acting in application of Article 15, paragraph 7, of the Covenant of the League of Nations, will immediately lend aid and assistance ...(19)'

More French commitments ARBITRATION CONVENTION BETWEEN GERMANY AND POLAND, INITIALLED ON 16 OCTOBER 1925

'(1) All disputes of every kind between Germany and Poland with regard to which the Parties are in conflict as to their respective rights, and which it may not be possible to settle amicably by the normal methods of diplomacy, shall be submitted for decision either to an arbitral tribunal or to the Permanent Court of International Justice …(20)'

In the Spring of next year (8 February 1926) the German Government formally asked to join the League of Nations, and on 8 September she was unanimously voted in. Briand enthusiastically declared: 'Arrière les canons, les fusils et les mitrailleuses! Arrière les voiles de deuil! … Place à l'arbitrage, à la sécurité et à la paix!'

Germany joins the League

Mussolini seemed to be the only real aggressor of the late twenties. On 26 November 1927, he signed a treaty with Albania, another a year later, and on 5 April 1927, a treaty with Hungary. All of them worried Yugoslavia, and the Little Entente.

On the international level, the Kellogg–Briand Pact, or the 'Pact of Paris', followed the Treaty of Locarno. This 'renunciation of War as an instrument of national policy', proposed by Briand, was arranged by US Secretary of State, Kellogg, and signed on 27 August 1928 in Paris. In all, sixty-five states eventually agreed to it.

Kellogg-Briand Peace Pact

But the Pact was no better than the League of Nations in its aim to prevent war. It concerned almost all types of wars—except so-called wars of 'self-defence'—yet made no provision for punishing those who started them.

Meanwhile, Germany again pressed hard for the evacuation of French troops from the Rhineland. The French at last agreed the occupation should end in 1930, instead of 1935 as laid down in the Treaty of Versailles—if Germany's financial obligations could be finally dealt with. Talks resulted in the Young Plan. Modifications were made to it after protests from Britain, but it was agreed that the last foreign troops would leave German soil by 30 June 1930.

But on 3 October 1929, Stresemann died, aged fifty-one, and in the same month, on 29 October, 'Black Friday', the crisis of economic confidence reached its terrible height in America's Wall Street. Post-war prosperity was over.

World economic slump

5 Depression and the Rise of the Führer

THERE were only two methods by which nations could pay interest on loans, or repay war debts. One was to pay in gold bullion, the other in goods. Gold payments were made until gold reserves began to run out, yet payment through goods was almost impossible because of the American tariff policy.

But America, too, needed to export. She found that she had to lend money for overseas buyers to purchase her goods. The situation was extremely artificial. Because American investors lacked the confidence to grant longer term loans, the situation was also extremely fragile. Loans were liable to sudden recall. Once investments began to be withdrawn, panic could quickly follow.

This delicate situation was, of course, aggravated by the reparations issue. The bubble burst in 1929. Late on 23–24 October, stockholders on Wall Street rushed to try and get back their investments. Once the panic had started, nothing could stop it. Prices began to fall. In three years, no less than 5,000 US banks closed down. American short-term loans were withdrawn.

In Germany, more and more people were thrown out of work, and protested angrily against reparation payments. Emergency measures had to be taken, including cuts in wages. The socialists objected, and on 28 March 1930, the Social Democratic Party left the German Coalition Government, issuing this appeal:

'... The Reich Government of Hermann Müller resigned on March 27, 1930. The struggle over unemployment insurance ... has led to an open crisis. Securing support for the huge army of ... unemployed is and remains an aim of Social Democracy, a reduction of benefits is the aim of the "Deutsche Volkspartei". This

The depression

Wall Street (1929)

Effects on Germany

51

Opposite Members of the Reichstag acclaim a speech by Hitler

contrast led to the crisis ... The social reaction wants to destroy unemployment insurance [to] force the worker to accept reductions in wages without opposition ...(21)'

Methods to end the reparations problem, including the Young Plan, stood even less chance of success. Who was to blame? In Germany at least, Hitler, with his campaign against the 'November criminals', seemed to be proved correct.

America tried to help with a proposal that all payments should be delayed for twelve months, to give everyone time to recover. But in fact reparations ended altogether in the early thirties. How much Germany had actually paid by then is difficult to judge, because in effect money had been pumped into the country in the form of the lavish short-term loans, so that it could flow out again as reparations. Germany had been kept economically afloat by her creditors because only by doing so could they be paid by her. It was a massive, and disastrous, financial circle.

The economic crisis had split the coalition government. (These coalitions were a result of the proportional representation system adopted by the Weimar Republic: no one group enjoyed a Reichstag majority, and so each had to join with others.) There was a search, by both the President and the rapidly changing Chancellors, for a way to govern, a government they hoped to control. Intrigue took over from politics, and Hitler was given his chance.

In July 1930, Brüning dissolved the Reichstag, hoping an election would return another which would give him better support. He was disappointed, for after the September elections his position was no stronger. He still depended on the authority of President Hindenburg, although he tried to avoid this by making use of presidential decrees issued under Article 48.

Adolf Hitler   At the beginning of 1932, Brüning opened talks with Hitler, to see whether he could use him. Hitler, in return, made impossible demands, and the talks broke down.

Yet Hitler and his party were still seen as a useful tool to gain a majority in the Reichstag. Once in firm power Brüning believed he would be able to manipulate Hitler. So began the long courtship of Hitler. He was disastrously underestimated. His speeches, and writings, including *Mein Kampf*, were ignored or ridiculed. So were warnings contained in speeches by other Nazi leaders.

Left Hitler and General Ludendorff. *Right* Franz von Papen as Chancellor failed to break Hitler's power

Goebbels had written in May 1928, for example, 'We go into the Reichstag in order to gather a supply of its own weapons in the arsenal of democracy. We will become Reichstag deputies in order to cripple the Weimar mentality with its own type of machinery. If democracy is so stupid as to provide us with free tickets and "per diem" payments for this injurious service, that is its own affair ... We come as enemies! We come like the wolf which breaks into the sheepfold! (22)' *Goebbels: wolves and sheep*

Democracy was indeed 'so stupid!' Brüning failed to win over Hitler, and had to resign on 30 May 1932. Hindenburg then tried to deal with Hitler, but he too failed. Franz von Papen was next made Chancellor. He tried to wear Hitler down by one Reichstag election after another, hoping that Nazi funds would run out. But Hitler knew that the longer he waited, the bigger the prize.

Some Germans did see the dangers. Hermann Dietrich, Brüning's former Finance Minister, warned, '... [Papen's Government] is Hitler's instrument and it has called forth dangers for the German people and Reich which we thought we had precluded through *A warning*

Left The Reichstag fire was probably started by van Lubbe (*right*) with Nazi backing

Presidential elections. A Nazi victory … betokens terrorism against people of other views, suppression of political freedom, unforeseeable economic experiments …(23)'

Papen and Hitler

Papen resigned, hoping to show Hindenburg how much he was needed. But he was replaced by Schleicher, who believed he could do better. He tried to use Strasser, who had apparently deserted to the Nazi cause, but Strasser, made Vice-Chancellor, failed to bring the Nazi party with him. Papen met Hitler secretly again. The political situation was becoming desperate, and on 28 January 1933, Schleicher had to confess to Hindenburg that he had failed. Papen was asked to find a new Government.

But at last Hitler was ready. He agreed to take office—on his own terms. On 30 January 1933, he became Chancellor. Even now the German leaders believed they had seized Hitler rather than that Hitler had seized them. How wrong they were.

The Reichstag fire

The Nazi leader, using the democratic machinery, strengthened his position. He called for elections. On 27 February the

Reichstag building caught fire, probably started by a young Dutch revolutionary, Marinus van Lubbe, with Nazi complicity. Hitler blamed the fire on the Communists and banned the party:

'In virtue of Article 48, paragraph 2, of the Constitution of the Reich, the following is ordered as a protection against Communist acts of violence imperilling the State:

'(1) Articles 114, 115, 117, 123, 124 and 153 of the Constitution of the German Reich are invalidated until further notice. Restrictions on personal freedom, on the right of free expression of opinion, including freedom of the press, and on rights of association, and assembling, encroachments on the secrecy of letters, post, telephone and telegraph, and orders for domiciliary searches and for the confiscation of or restrictions on property, are therefore permissible even outside the legal bounds otherwise set for this purpose ...'

So not only the Communists, but all Hitler's political opponents were stifled. And yet in the elections of 5 March Hitler's National Socialists still only won 43·9 per cent of the votes, barely a majority. He still needed more power. He therefore put forward his 'Law to relieve the Distress of the People and the Reich', or the 'Enabling Law', on 24 March, which would in effect give him dictatorial powers. *Hitler as dictator*

The law was vigorously resisted by the Social Democrats in the Reichstag, who voted against it. Otto Wels, the Socialist leader, said in the debate, 'Freedom and life can be taken away from us, but not our honour. After the persecutions lately endured by the Socialist Party, no one will require or expect it to support the Enabling Act ...

'Never, since a German Reichstag has existed, has the control of public affairs through the chosen representatives of the people been eliminated to such an extent as is now the case and will still more be so as the result of the new Enabling Act ...

'At this historic moment we German Social Democrats solemnly affirm our allegiance to the principles of humanity and justice, of freedom and Socialism ...(24)'

But the Centre, fobbed off with promises from Hitler, went along with it. Hitler promised them: 'The number of cases when an inherent necessity to use the law [would be] limited'. *Opposition to Hitler*

The Law was passed:

'(1) Laws of the Reich can be passed not only in the manner

prescribed by the Constitution of the Reich but also by the Government ...

'(2) Laws passed by the Government of the Reich can be at variance with the Constitution of the Reich so long as they do not deal with the actual institution of the Reichstag or of the Reichsrat. The rights of the President of the Reich remain untouched.

'(3) Laws passed by the Government of the Reich will be drawn up by the Chancellor of the Reich ...(25)'

Hitler bans non-Nazi parties

Hitler went further, bending the legal machinery of the parliamentary system to its limits. On 14 July the 'Law forbidding the Formation of Parties' was passed:

'(1) The only political party existing in Germany is the National Socialist German Workers' Party.

'(2) Whoever takes steps to maintain the organized existence of another political party or to form a new political party will ... be punished with penal servitude up to three years or with imprisonment from six months to three years (26).'

Fast on its heels came the 'Law to secure the Unity of the Party and the State', on 1 December 1933, which really completed Hitler's *gleichschaltung* (take over) of the German parliamentary structure:

'(1) As a result of the victory of the National Socialist revolution, the National Socialist German Workers' Party is the custodian of the German national sentiment ...

'(2) In order to guarantee the closest cooperation between the officials of the Party and of the SA and the public authorities, the Deputy of the Leader and the Chief of Staff of the SA shall be members of the Government of the Reich ...'

Meanwhile Hitler had mastered the old, probably senile, President Hindenburg. Key Nazis were put into the most important jobs.

'*Sharpen the spear*'

Goebbels was made Minister of Propaganda. Long before he had described his techniques. Writing in his newspaper *Der Angriff* in 1929, when he had been appointed chief of the Nazi party propaganda, Goebbels declared: 'To spring ice-cold onto your opponent's back, feel him out, find where his vulnerable spot lies, sharpen the spear with careful calculation, thrust it with well-directed aim into the enemy's weak point—and then perhaps say with a friendly smile: Excuse me neighbour, there was nothing else I could do! (27)'

Himmler was put in charge of the police, reorganized under the vicious control of the Secret State Police—the Gestapo or SS. Also, in October 1933, the German Government announced with 'great regret' its decision to quit the Disarmament Conference and the League of Nations.

These were the official reasons for her withdrawal: 'Filled with the sincere desire to accomplish the work of the peaceful internal reconstruction of our nation and of its political and economic life, former German Governments, trusting in the grant of a dignified equality of rights, declared their willingness to enter the League of Nations and to take part in the Disarmament Conference.

'In this connexion Germany suffered a bitter disappointment.

'In spite of our readiness to carry through German disarmament ... other Governments could not decide to redeem the pledges signed by them in the Peace Treaty.

'By the deliberate refusal of real moral and material equality of rights to Germany, the German nation and its Governments have been profoundly humiliated.

'After the German Government had declared, as a result of the equality of rights expressly laid down on December 11, 1932, that it was again prepared to take part in the Disarmament Conference, the German Foreign Minister and our delegates were informed ... that this equality of rights could no longer be granted to present-day Germany ...

'As the German Government regards this action as an unjust and humiliating discrimination against the German nation, it is not in a position to continue, as an outlawed and second-class nation, to take part in negotiations which could only lead to further arbitrary results.

'While the German Government again proclaims its unshaken desire for peace, it declares to its great regret that in view of these imputations, it must leave the Disarmament Conference. It will also announce its departure from the League of Nations (28).'

The Führer next tightened his grip on his own Nazi Party at home. Some extremists among his storm troopers—*Sturmabteilung*, known as Brownshirts or the SA—were pressing for true socialism in a 'second revolution', as opposed to the dictatorship Hitler was planning for himself.

As early as July 1933, Hitler had warned, 'I will suppress every attempt to disturb the existing order as ruthlessly as I will deal with the so-called Second Revolution. Whoever raises his head against the established authority of the State will be severely treated, whatever his position.'

The warning was defied by Röhm, the SA leader, who declared on 18 April 1934, 'The militant in the Brown Shirt from the first day pledged himself to the path of revolution, and he will not deviate by a hairbreadth until our ultimate goal has been achieved.' Röhm even left out the usual 'Heil Hitler!' at the end of his speech.

So, on 30 June 1934, known afterwards as 'the Night of the Long Knives', Hitler struck out. SA leaders including Röhm and Heines were brutally murdered, with Hitler using the alleged threat of a Röhm 'plot' as an excuse. Other likely rivals were also exterminated —Strasser, Schleicher, and Klausner, Chief of the Rhenish Catholic Party. In all, between 5,000 and 7,000 people were 'liquidated'.

In July, Hitler explained his actions to the Reichstag. He was far from apologetic: '... The necessity for acting with lightning speed meant that in this decisive hour I had very few men with me ... Although only a few days before I had been prepared to exercise clemency, at this hour there was no place for any such consideration. Mutinies are suppressed in accordance with laws of iron which are eternally the same.

'If anyone reproaches me and asks why I did not resort to the regular Courts of Justice for conviction of the offenders, then all that I can say to him is this: In this hour I was responsible for the fate of the German people, and thereby I became the supreme Justiciar of the German people ... I did not wish to deliver up the Young Reich to the fate of the Old Reich. I gave the order to shoot those who were the ringleaders in this treason ...(29)'

The army, disliking and jealous of the SA, was implicated in the purge, and was now bound closer to Hitler. At the same time, Hitler assured the army leaders they would not be interfered with, and he promised them rearmament. And so, when Hindenburg died on 2 August 1934, the army chiefs were content Hitler should take his place, merging the offices of Chancellor and President.

Hitler was now undisputed dictator of the German nation. He played on just the right feeling of militarism, nationalism and bitter-

Opposite: top left Hitler awaits a Freedom Day procession in Cologne. *Right* Fieldmarshal Blomberg, sacked by Hitler. *Below* Hitler takes the salute during a march-past of Brownshirts

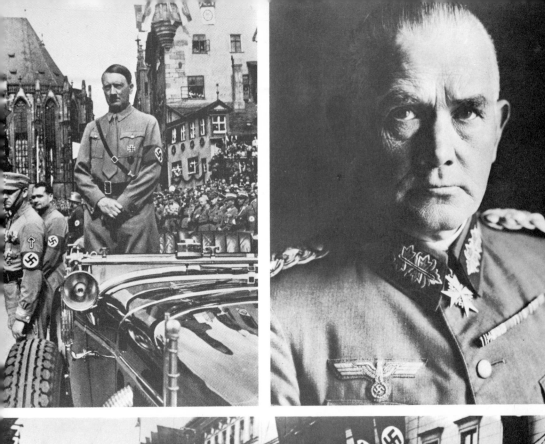

ness among influential sections of the German people.

Otto Spengler was one of the non-Nazi writers who created the violent atmosphere which helped Hitler to power. He wrote (1924): '... He who cannot hate is no man, and history is made by men ... The fact that we as Germans are at last able to hate is one of the few outgrowths of this period which would provide some surety for our future ...(30)'

In 1931 Spengler remarked, '... We have been born into this time and we must bravely pursue to its end the path assigned to us. No other one exists. It is our duty to hold out on the lost post without hope, without rescue. To hold out like that Roman soldier whose bones were found outside a gate in Pompeii, who died because when Vesuvius erupted no one remembered to relieve him. That is greatness, that is what it means to have breeding ...(31)'

And two years later, '[the pacifists say] no more war [but] battle is the source of life, it is life itself; and even the most pitiable pacifist cannot altogether succeed in rooting desire for it out of his soul ...(32)'

Everything was going Hitler's way. His final moves were to be made later, against the army leaders. Fritsch and Blomberg were thrown out, the first after a false charge of homosexuality had been made against him, the second because he had married a prostitute. The Generals, who had once believed themselves above politics, were to swear allegiance not just to the State—but to the State's political leader, ex-Corporal Adolf Hitler.

6 The Middle Years: 1933-36

WITH the effects of the economic crisis and the growing fear of Germany, France went through growing political confusion, riots, resignations, and 'revolving door' governments. The crisis of 6 February 1934, for example, paralysed France internationally and encouraged Hitler. The atmosphere of French politics deteriorated rapidly since the Stavisky affair in January 1934, when the suicide of this financier, a fraudilist, compromised members of the Government. In February, extremist right-wing groups attacked the Chamber of Deputies, issuing this proclamation:

'France for the French! Take your brooms and sweep out the rubbish! We have had enough of this! In all towns, in all villages, you, members of the "Solidarité Française" must demonstrate ... against this grotesque regime, against the parliamentary profiteers ... The Government must be made to realize that the people of *France* have wakened and that they are determined to put an end to the reign of international revolutionaries and corrupt politicians (33).'

For a time, Louis Barthou put life back into French foreign policy, but he died with King Alexander of Yugoslavia, victims of assassins' bullets, when the King was visiting France in October 1934. According to Lord Avon, 'These were the first shots of the Second World War.'

The sinister Laval took over the French Foreign Ministry, telling the press he intended to come to terms with Germany and Italy. On 3 December he made a bargain with Germany over the Saar coalmines, and three days later told the League of Nations Council that France would not oppose the return of the Saar to Hitler. In Jan-

Stavisky affair (1934)

Pierre Laval

The beginning of the Abyssinian campaign; Italian troops march off to embark for Africa

uary, after a massive Nazi propaganda campaign, ninety per cent of the Saarlanders voted to return to Germany. Hitler and Goebbels congratulated themselves, and non-Nazi Europe grew more alarmed.

But alarm was one thing, positive action another. On 15 March 1935, the French Chamber of Deputies voted against stepping up military service in France to two years. The very next day Hitler, in defiance of the Versailles Treaty, brought back German conscription (see Chapter 9). It was a strange contrast. Thanks to pressure from Herriot, the French signed a pact with Russia on 2 May, saying that if either power were attacked the other would come to its rescue. But the rift in French politics continued.

Mussolini invades Abyssinia

Both the Fascist and Nazi camps were becoming more warlike. In October 1935, Mussolini marched Italian troops into Abyssinia, to reduce political discontent and economic deterioration at home. He used the pretext of a minor clash which had taken place in December 1934 on the borders of Abyssinia and Italian Somaliland. Some 30,000 men were conscripted for the war. At least it was something for the unemployed to do, and the economy certainly benefited from the war production.

The Foreign Ministers of England and France, Hoare (*left*) and Laval
(*right*), both acquiesced in the Italian attack on Abyssinia

The Italian aggression showed up the weaknesses of the League of
Nations. On 10 October the League Assembly voted to take collective measures against Italy, but its sanctions were not backed by
force.

This did not go unnoticed in Germany. As an article in the
Münchener Zeitung was to say on 16 May 1936: 'Today all
Abyssinia is irrevocably, fully, and finally Italian alone. This being
so, neither Geneva nor London can have any doubt that only the
use of extraordinary force can drive the Italians out of Abyssinia.
But neither the power nor the courage to use force is at hand (34).'

How did Britain and France react to this crime? On 10 December
1935 their Foreign Ministers—Hoare and Laval—proposed carving
up Abyssinia between Italy and the Emperor:

Hoare-Laval proposals

'(*I*) Exchange of Territories. The Governments of the United
Kingdom and France agree to recommend to His Majesty the
Emperor of Ethiopia the acceptance of the following exchanges of
territory between Ethiopia and Italy.

'(*a*) Cession to Italy of eastern Tigre …

'(*b*) Rectification of frontiers between the Danakil country and

63

The Council of the League of Nations hears a speech by von Ribbentrop
in March 1936

Eritrea …

'(*c*) Rectification of frontiers between the Ogaden and Italian Somaliland …

'(*d*) Ethiopia will receive an outlet to the sea with full sovereign rights. It seems that this outlet should be formed preferably by the cession, to which Italy would agree, of the port of Assab and of a strip of territory giving access to this port along the frontier of French Somaliland …(35).'

This scheme, approved by the British Cabinet on 9 December, so assisted Mussolini it eventually had to be scrapped. Hoare resigned.

Hitler invades
Rhineland

But Hitler had taken the point. Using the pretext of the Franco–Soviet military pact, he announced on 7 March 1936 that he had sent armies into the Rhineland. It was a dramatic move, Hitler's first major territorial aggression. No one did anything about it. France was in endless political turmoil, with more elections due in six months. In Britain, opinion was confused.

Hitler published his reasons. Here is an extract from the German 'Memorandum respecting the Termination of the Treaty of Locarno and the Re-occupation of the Rhineland, 7 March 1936':

'... The latest debates and decisions of the French Parliament have shown that France, in spite of the German representations, is determined to put the pact with the Soviet Union definitively into force.

'The German Government have continually emphasized during the negotiations of the last years their readiness to observe and fulfil all the obligations arising from the Rhine Pact as long as the other contracting parties were ready on their side to maintain the pact. This obvious and essential condition can no longer be regarded as fulfilled by France.'

Now, it went on, 'Germany regards herself for her part as no longer bound by this dissolved treaty ... In accordance with the fundamental right of a nation to secure its frontiers and ensure its possibilities of defence, the German Government have today restored the full and unrestricted sovereignty of Germany in the demilitarized zone of the Rhineland ...(36)'

Many believed it was even right for Germany to re-take what was, after all, her own territory. This belief was to be one of the main principles behind the policy of appeasement.

Churchill thought the opposite. On 6 April he gave the House of Commons an ominous warning: 'Herr Hitler has torn up the treaties and has garrisoned the Rhineland. His troops are there, and there they are going to stay. All this means that the Nazi regime has gained a new prestige in Germany and in all the neighbouring countries. But more than that, Germany is now fortifying the Rhine zone or is about to fortify it ... I do not doubt that the whole of the German frontier opposite to France is to be fortified as strongly and as speedily as possible. Three, four, or six months will certainly see a barrier of enormous strength. What will be the diplomatic and strategic consequences of that? (37)'

Churchill's warning

7 The Military Rehearsal— The Spanish Civil War

THE COLLAPSE of General Primo de Rivera in 1930, military dictator Spanish troubles in Spain since 1923, threw Spain into confusion, made worse by the abdication of King Alfonso XIII and the economic slump. The confusion continued throughout the early 1930s. The 1936 elections were won by parties comprising the Popular Front, put forward by the Communists. But in the opposing Monarchist group was the CEDA party—the Confederación Española de Derechas Autonoma—still the largest single party of all. No one knew what would happen.

On 13 July 1936, the police murdered Calvo Sotelo, the Monarchist leader, in revenge for a murder of one of their own officers. And in the riots which followed, General Franco travelled from the Canary Islands to begin his battle against the Republican Government.

Two days later he issued his first manifesto: 'Spaniards! The Franco's call to arms Nation calls to her defence all of you who feel a holy love for Spain, you who, in the ranks of the Army and the Navy, have made a profession of faith in the service of our country, you who have sworn to defend her with your lives against her enemies …

'Gravest offences are committed in the cities and the countryside while the forces of public order remain in their quarters, corroded by the desperation caused by [the necessity] of blindly obeying leaders who intend to dishonour them. The Army, the Navy, and other armed organizations are the target of the vilest and most slanderous attacks precisely on the part of those who ought to protect their good name.

'States of emergency and alert are only imposed to gag the people,

67

Opposite: top left King Alfonso XIII of Spain and his Queen. *Right* General Franco making a speech at Burgos in 1936, *below* Franco at the Catalonian front in 1939

to keep Spain ignorant of what goes on outside everybody's own city or town, and to imprison pretended political enemies.

'The Constitution is gravely violated by all ...

'The Magistracy, whose independence is guaranteed by the Constitution, is weakened and undermined by persecution ...

'Electoral pacts made at the expense of the integrity of the Country, combined with attacks on government offices and strongrooms to falsify election returns ...(38).'

Civil war   Civil war had broken out, confused, complicated, with neither side completely in the right or wrong. As Churchill wrote in the *Evening Standard* on 7 August 1937, 'The worst quarrels only arise when both sides are equally in the right and in the wrong. Here, on the one hand, the passions of a poverty-stricken and backward proletariat demand the overthrow of Church, State, and property, and the inauguration of a Communist regime. On the other hand, the patriotic, religious, and "bourgeois" forces, under the leadership of the Army, and sustained by the countryside in many provinces, are marching to re-establish order by setting up a military dictatorship ...'

French   Both sides at once sought foreign support. The Republicans
attitude   turned to Blum, who had been in power in France for just six months, and Franco appealed to Hitler and Mussolini. These two, justifying their intervention as part of their battle against Communism, obliged. Blum on the other hand, proposed on 2 August that France, Italy and Britain should agree to stay out of the war.

The Dictators   Stalin said, on 23 August, that he would not become involved, but in mid-October Russian military aid did in fact begin to arrive in Spain. Italy and Germany, on August 21 and 24 respectively, also declared they would not become involved, but the statements were worthless. So the 'Non-Intervention' Committee, set up in September 1936 and representing twenty-seven states, meant very little— although Blum, a pacifist, and Baldwin, were determined not to become entangled.

The Republicans appealed to the League of Nations on 27 November 1936, and in Resolutions on 12 December and 29 May 1937, the League condemned the foreign powers for stepping in. But as with the Italian invasion of Abyssinia, words could not be turned into action. This was what the League voted:

Left Hitler and Mussolini in 1934. *Right* Léon Blum, leader of the French Socialists

First resolution

'Confirming the principles and recommendations set forth in its resolution of December 12, 1936, and, in particular, the duty of every State to respect the territorial integrity and political independence of other States …

'(1) Observes with regret that the development of the situation in Spain does not seem to suggest that the steps taken by Governments on the recommendations of the Council have as yet had the full effect desired …

Second resolution

'(1) Profoundly moved by the horrors resulting from the use of certain methods of warfare, condemns the employment, in the Spanish struggle, of methods contrary to international law and the bombing of open towns;

'(2) Desires to emphasize its high appreciation of the efforts of unofficial institutions and certain Governments to save civilians, especially women and children, from these terrible dangers (39).'

It was hardly enough to be 'profoundly moved'. Virtually the only time a positive step was taken to restrict intervention during the war,

League of Nations 'profoundly moved'

69

was the decision by France and Britain, at the Nyons Conference, September 1937, to send warships to the Mediterranean to stop Italian submarines preying on supposed Republican ships. This action was an immediate success. But Chamberlain, who became Prime Minister on 28 May, was—like Baldwin—against Britain taking any further part.

From the very start, however, Germany was involved. Thirty *Junkers* transport aircraft ferried Franco's troops from Morocco to Spain in the opening stages of the war. Then followed the notorious German Condor Air Legion, which gained valuable experience in dive-bombing techniques, for example at Durango on 1 March 1937, and Guernica on 26 April. The bombing of Guernica inspired Pablo Picasso—himself a Spaniard—to paint one of his greatest paintings, passionately opposing war.

German intervention

But German military aid was only on a small scale. The Condor Legion only comprised four fighter-bomber, four fighter, one reconnaissance and two seaplane squadrons detached from the *Luftwaffe*. In addition there was tank support to Franco, but it only consisted of one battalion. The rest of the military assistance was made up of weapons shipments. Even this was too much for some German Army leaders, who felt Germany did not have enough to spare.

Beck anxiously told Hitler in January 1937, 'If it should come to developments of a warlike nature in May or June of 1937, our position would be inconceivable.'

Yet, when the Spanish Civil War reached a stalemate at the end of 1937, the amount of foreign help each side could obtain became decisive. And Franco, with this German assistance, and with the Italian tanks and 'volunteer' troops totalling 100,000 men, was able gradually to wear down the Republicans. By the end of March 1939, Madrid itself had fallen. Stalin, seeing the end, had already withdrawn the official Communist contribution. The International Brigade, recruited from volunteers from various countries, and numbering at the most 40,000 men, stayed longer, but dwindled. France and Britain had already recognized Franco on 27 February 1939.

Franco's victory

Hitler had helped inflict another blow to democracy in Europe. Britain and France had suffered another disgrace. Moreover, stronger links between Italy and Germany had been forged. During

Rome-Berlin Axis

71

Opposite The Spanish Civil War; a father instructs his daughter in rifle drill the war Mussolini had given this relationship the sinister name of 'Axis', saying on 1 November 1936, 'This vertical line between Rome and Berlin is not a partition but rather an axis around which can revolve all those European states with a will to collaboration and peace.'

But it was a one-sided relationship. Hitler used Mussolini, rather than vice-versa. Italy needed Germany, and this need was to become greater. As Hitler wrote to Mussolini on 6 March 1940: 'The outcome of this war will also decide the future of Italy. If this future is considered in your country in terms of merely perpetuating the existence of a European state of modest pretensions, then I am wrong. But if this future is considered in terms of a guarantee of the existence of the Italian people from a historical, geopolitical and moral point of view, or according to the rights of your people, those who are fighting Germany today will be your enemies too (40).'

Franco and his wife acclaimed by Nationalist sympathizers

8 Anschluss

AS MACHINE-GUNS crackled in Spain, breaches began to appear in central Europe and Nazi jackboots were ready to step in. In Czechoslovakia, Konrad Henlein had formed his *Sudetendeutsche Heimatfront* party, the SHF, in October 1933, and the SHF, with financial help from Berlin, had become the largest party in the 1935 Czech elections. In 1935 Thomas Masaryk resigned as President, and Beneš took his place; Beneš was a supporter of the Franco–Russian treaty and a natural target for Hitler's anti-Communist campaign.

Hitler saw Czechoslovakia and Austria as the essential core of the *Mitteleuropa* (Middle Europe) which he planned as the basis of his German Empire. On the very first page of *Mein Kampf* he had written, 'German Austria must return to the German Motherland.' Germany needed *liebensraum* (living space)—Poland, White Russia and the Ukraine. First, Germany must take Austria and Czechoslovakia, even if this meant war. *'Middle Europe'*

Engelbert Dollfüss had tried to make Austria stronger in April 1934 by giving her a new constitution. But in July 1934, he had been murdered by the Nazis, who seized the Vienna radio station and tried to carry out a *coup*. This failed. Opposition was still too strong. Mussolini, not yet an ally of Hitler, mobilized his troops. *Dollfüss*

In January 1934, Mussolini's foreign affairs adviser, Suvich, visited Austria as a warning to Germany, saying on 21 January: '... If she [Austria] is to fulfil, in the interests of all, the missions accorded her by centuries-old tradition and geographical situation, the normal conditions of independence and peaceful life must first of all be secured. That is the standpoint which Italy has long maintained in regard to both political and economic conditions on the *Italy warns Germany* basis of unchangeable principles (41).'

German secret plans On 21 May 1936, Hitler told the Reichstag, 'Germany neither intends nor wishes to interfere in the internal affairs of Austria, to annex Austria, or to conclude an *Anschluss*.'

This was followed by a much-publicized pact with Austria, but at the same time, Hitler's General Staff was secretly preparing 'Case Otto' for the occupation of Austria. More plans were worked out in June 1937. Ominously, Hitler took over Supreme Command of the German Army himself on 4 February 1938. Pressure against Austria was stepped up.

Ribbentrop took over from Neurath as German Foreign Minister, and on 14 February Hitler approved Keitel's suggestion that the German Army should appear to be preparing action against Austria. As a result of this pressure, the Austrians 'agreed' to a 'closer understanding' between the two countries.

On 20 February, Hitler anounced to the Reichstag: 'I am happy to be able to tell you, gentlemen, that during the past few days a further understanding has been reached with a country that is particularly close to us for many reasons. The Reich and German Austria are bound together not only because they share a long history and a common culture ... The idea and the intentions were to bring about a relaxation of the strain in our relations with one another by giving under the existing legislation the same legal rights to citizens holding National-Socialist views, as are enjoyed by the other citizens of German Austria ... after all, it is the interest of the whole German people, whose sons we all are, wherever we may have been born (42).'

Anschluss On 11–12 March German troops marched over the border and German tank units rumbled into Austria. *Anschluss* took place. In Britain, Prime Minister Chamberlain was embarrassed by the news as he was holding a dinner in honour of von Ribbentrop, the German Ambassador in London due to leave to take up his Foreign Minister's appointment.

By now, Hitler and Mussolini were reaching agreement. Unlike the situation in 1934, Mussolini would not try to get in the way. The Führer and the Duce were partners.

Jede Stimme am 29. März: Eine Waffe

9 Armies and Appeasement

BY NOW the German Army had been completely recreated, and with *Blitzkreig* it the deadly doctrine of *blitzkrieg* (lightning war). The essence of this doctrine was speed and surprise. The means to undertake it had been shown long before, in restricted form at Cambrai in 1917 and on 18 July and 8 August 1918 at Soissons and Amiens—the tank. Tanks, working in conjunction with air power, would resurrect Schlieffen's pre-1914 strategy—a strategy of sudden encirclement and annihilation of Germany's enemies.

In the development of the new German army and of the *blitzkrieg* doctrine, the Germans were actually helped by the Versailles disarmament clauses. Being defeated and disarmed, the Germans had to make a fresh start, with fewer illusions about earlier military strategy, and with a clean military cupboard to be re-stocked. The allies, on the other hand, rested on their laurels. Mistakes were not analyzed, equipment was not sufficiently replaced.

In Germany, influential officers like Guderian—Hitler's first Mobile Troops commander—believed that since Germany's forces were relatively small, they needed a strategy of mobility, surprise, and concentration. Guderian had read the works of the English tank advocates, Fuller and Liddell-Hart. During 1929–30, Liddell-Hart evolved his concept of the deep penetration of opposing forces. This concept was directly adopted by Guderian and the other German strategists for the *blitzkrieg* idea.

Following the secret talks with Russia, military air force and tank *Krupp* warfare training centres were set up on Russian soil in the 1920s; the tank centre, near Kazan, began operating in 1929. In 1933 the German arms firm of Krupp started its first regular tank production

77

Opposite Hitler addressing a Nazi party meeting at Frankfurt in March 1936

Left Liddell-Hart the English strategist and advocate of tanks, whose ideas were successfully adopted by the Germans. *Right* A German armoured car.

Churchill's warning

Germany comes into the open

programme, under the label of an 'Agricultural Tractor Service'.

Some of the foreign observers were beginning to grow anxious. Churchill told the House of Commons in November 1933, 'We read of large importations of scrap iron and nickel and war metals, quite out of the ordinary. We read all the news which accumulates of the military spirit which is rife throughout the country; we see that a philosophy of blood-lust is being inculcated into their youth to which no parallel can be found since the days of barbarism.'

That autumn came the first experiment in the system evolved by Seeckt in the 1920s for trebling the size of the German Army, and with Hitler's takeover of power, rearmament was speeded up. Hitler strongly supported the organization of the tank units—the Panzer Corps. On 9 March 1935 the German air force was officially announced. A week later, Hitler denounced the military clauses of the Versailles Treaty:

'When in November 1918, the German People, trusting in the promises given in President Wilson's Fourteen Points, grounded arms after four and a half year's honourable resistance in a war whose outbreak they had never desired, they believed they had rendered a service not only to tormented humanity, but also to a great idea ...

'Germany has ... fulfilled the disarmament conditions imposed

78

upon her ... the German people had the right to expect the redemption also by the other side of obligations undertaken ... But while Germany as one party to the Treaty had fulfilled its obligations, the redemption of the obligation on the part of the second partner to the Treaty failed to become a fact. That means: the High Contracting Parties of the former victor States, have one-sidedly divorced themselves from the obligations of the Versailles Treaty. Not alone did they refrain from disarming ... No. Not even was there a halt in the armaments race, on the contrary, the increase of armaments ... became evident ...'

Hitler went on, 'The world ... has again resumed its cries of war, just as though there never had been a World War nor the Versailles Treaty ... In the midst of these highly armed warlike States ... Germany was, militarily speaking, in a vacuum, defencelessly at the mercy of every threatening danger.

'In these circumstances,' he concluded, 'the German Government considers it impossible still longer to refrain from taking the necessary measures for the security of the Reich or even to hide the knowledge thereof from other Nations ...(43)'

Hitler now brought back military service. The *Truppengeneralstab* threw off its disguise and assumed its real title of General Staff. *League protests*

In April, the League of Nations anxiously discussed Germany's breach of the Versailles Treaty, and nineteen countries lodged protests, accepting recommendations made by the French.

These recommendations were:

'(1) That the scrupulous respect of all treaty obligations is a fundamental principle of international life and an essential condition of the maintenance of peace;

'(2) That it is an essential principle of the law of nations that no Power can liberate itself from the engagements of a treaty nor modify the stipulations thereof unless with the consent of the other contracting parties;

'(3) That the promulgation of the Military Law of March 16, 1935, by the German Government conflicts with the above principles;

'(5) That this unilateral action, by introducing a new disturbing element into the international situation, must necessarily appear to be a threat to European security ...

'(*I*) Declares that Germany has failed in the duty which lies upon all the members of the international community to respect the undertakings which they have contracted, and condemns any unilateral repudiation of international obligations ...

'(*III*) Considering that the unilateral repudiation of international obligations may endanger the very existence of the League of Nations as an organization for maintaining peace and promoting security, decides:

'That such repudiation ... should, in the event of its having relation to undertakings concerning the security of people and the maintenance of peace in Europe, call into play all appropriate measures on the part of Members of the League and within the framework of the Covenant ...(44)'

But as Churchill wrote, 'How vain was all their voting without the readiness of any single Power or any group of Powers to contemplate the use of *force*, even in the last resort! (45)'

Stresa
Declaration
Also in April, worried British, French and Italian Ministers held a meeting at Stresa. According to their Final Declaration, 'The three Powers, the object of whose policy is the collective maintenance of peace within the framework of the League of Nations, find themselves in complete agreement in opposing, by all practicable means, any unilateral repudiation of treaties which may endanger the peace of Europe, and will act in close and cordial collaboration ...

'The Representatives of the Governments of Italy, France and the United Kingdom have examined at Stresa the general European situation in the light of the results of the exchanges of views which have taken place in recent weeks.

'(2) The information which they have received has confirmed their view that the negotiations should be pursued for the development which is desired in security in Eastern Europe ...

'(5) In approaching the problem of armaments ... it was regretfully recognized that the method of unilateral repudiation adopted by the German Government ... had undermined public confidence in the security of a peaceful order. Moreover, the magnitude of the declared programme of German rearmament ... had invalidated the quantitative assumptions upon which efforts for disarmament had hitherto been based and shaken hopes by which those efforts were inspired (46).'

Marshal Pétain, French Minister of War, whose policy of defensive fortifications proved a disaster

At that time, Italy was still apart from Germany, and it was Britain's policy to keep her so. But as for Germany herself, the 'all practicable means' to restrain her did not include the use of force. Britain and France were militarily unprepared.

Meanwhile in May 1935 the name of *Reichswehr* (State Army) for the Germany Army was changed to *Wehrmacht* (Armed Strength), and in October 1935 the first three complete Panzer divisions were organized.

Military matters

In France, military doctrine rested upon a defensive strategy, encouraged by Marshal Pétain. The offensive strategy laid down by Foch and his disciples before 1914 had, according to the experts, been proved wrong in the First World War. The war had shown that France must put her trust in fortifications. She must therefore build defensive fortresses, ready for any enemy foolhardy enough to attack—and if the enemy should be Germany, then disarmed, France would have plenty of time to prepare while the Germans rebuilt their forces.

Gradually, pressure for a mechanized *corps de bataille* (battle corps) did have some success. But the emphasis was still on strong reliance on the Maginot defensive line. In 1935, when Gamelin—Chief of General Staff—was warned of the situation in Germany by the French Ambassador in Berlin, he replied, 'Aircraft do not decide the outcome of a battle ... Armoured divisions are too heavy and cumbersome. They may penetrate our lines, but the lips of the gash will close up behind them and we shall crush them with our reserves (47)'

So France still believed that, because static defences had proved so invulnerable in 1914, they would again. Germany was meanwhile evolving a plan to break through the trench warfare deadlock, and the French defensive policy meant that the French forces were tied to their own territory, at a time when France was committing herself heavily to alliances in East and West Europe.

British 'Peace hypothesis'
Nor could Britain offer any help, even if she wanted to. The desire for disarmament after the war had continued. Lloyd George's Coalition War Cabinet had, in the summer of 1919, assumed that: 'The British Empire will not be engaged in any great war during the next ten years, and that no expeditionary force will be required.'

This 'peace hypothesis' or 'Ten Year Rule' was reaffirmed at intervals, in relation to separate Service departments, even by Churchill. On 5 July 1928 the Government agreed with Churchill that, 'The basis of estimates for the Service Departments should rest upon the statement that there would be no major war for a period of ten years, and that this basis should advance from day to day, but that the assumption should be reviewed every year by the Committee of Imperial Defence (48).'

Weak British forces
It was laid down in 1923 that the British air force should have fifty-two squadrons by 1928. But by 1934 the RAF still only had forty-two. The Army was the worst sufferer from economies. Allocations for the purchase and maintenance of army weapons and war stores between 1923 and 1933 only averaged about £2 million a year. Money, where available, was not spent on tanks—despite pressure from experts such as Fuller and Liddell-Hart, the latter with his ambitious 'indirect approach', and 'expanding torrent' strategies. Liddell-Hart wanted independent armoured striking units to punch a hole in the enemy defensive lines, through which

forces could be poured to encircle and trap the opposition.

Colonel J. F. C. Fuller said the static stalemate of 1914–18 would be changed by the tanks—'half an inch of steel'. Battles would take place between opposing tank units, with the infantry playing only a minor role. 'Well in the the rear, on some anti-tank hill top, will be congregated the infantry, loudly applauding this excellent sport (49).'

But neither Fuller's more extreme views nor Liddell-Hart's sensible suggestions received adequate support. The cavalry school was still too strong, money was short and had to be shared with the RAF, and disarmament was still believed the correct policy.

But in February 1932 the Chiefs of Staff did denounce the 'Ten Year Rule', and it was revoked on 23 March by the MacDonald Government. Yet eighteen months passed before the Cabinet appointed a Defence Requirements Committee to 'prepare a programme for meeting our worst deficiencies.'

In the Commons in May 1932, Churchill had given his first warning of the dangers of disarmament. He had been provoked by the policy of the Government which sought to reduce French arms to match the size of the German forces: 'I should very much regret to see any approximation in military strength between Germany and France. Those who speak of that as though it were right, or even a question of fair dealing, altogether underrate the gravity of the European situation ... I regretted to hear the Under-Secretary say that we were only the fifth air Power, and that the ten-year programme was suspended for another year.

Churchill: 'A poor boast'

'I was sorry to hear him boast that the Air Ministry had not laid down a single new unit this year. All these ideas are being increasingly stultified by the march of events, and we should be well advised to concentrate upon our air defences (50).'

Churchill was still very much alone. The German demands for the removal of all rearmament restrictions met with approval in Britain. *The Times* described it as 'the timely redress of inequality'.

The Oxford University Union passed its famous resolution in 1933, 'This House will in no circumstances fight for its King and Country', and at the East Fulham parliamentary by-election on 25 October a pacifist programme increased the Socialist vote by nearly 9,000. The successful candidate, Mr Wilmot, said: 'The British

'King and Country'

people demand ... that the British Government shall give a lead to the whole world by initiating immediately a policy of general disarmament.' Lansbury, the leader of the Labour Party, said all nations must 'disarm to the level of Germany as a preliminary to total disarmament'.

Yet, also in October 1933, Hitler withdrew from the Disarmament Conference and the League of Nations.

Vote of Censure

In Britain the mood against British rearmament continued, despite warnings from Churchill and despite Hitler's boast to Sir John Simon, the Foreign Secretary, in 1934 that the German Air Force was now equal to Britain's. In July 1934, the Labour Party, supported by the Liberals, moved a Vote of Censure upon the Government. The motion (which failed) regretted that: 'His Majesty's Government should enter upon a policy of rearmament neither necessitated by any new commitments nor calculated to add to the security of the nation, but certain to jeopardize the prospects of international disarmament and to encourage a revival of dangerous and wasteful competition in preparation for war.'

Labour

Mr. Clement Attlee, speaking for the Opposition, said: 'We deny the need for increased air armaments ... We deny the proposition that an increased British air force will make for the peace of the world, and we reject altogether the (German) claim to parity ...(51).'

Conservative

Baldwin uncomfortable

The Baldwin Cabinet grew more alarmed about German policy, but as Baldwin said in 1936, in a Commons reply to Churchill, 'My position as the leader of a great party was not altogether a comfortable one. I asked myself what chance was there—when that feeling that was given expression to in Fulham was common throughout the country—what chance was there within the next year or two of that feeling being so changed that the country would give a mandate for rearmament?'

He added, 'Supposing I had gone to the country and said that Germany was rearming, and that we must rearm, does anybody think that this pacific democracy would have rallied to that cry at that moment? I cannot think of anything that would have made the loss of the election from my point of view more certain (52).'

Anglo-German Naval Agreement

But some steps were taken in 1935. In July a Defence Policy and Requirements Committee was instructed 'to keep the defence situation as a whole constantly under review so as to ensure that our

Opposite Stanley Baldwin, the British Prime Minister

defensive arrangements and our foreign policy are in line'. In the same year came the Anglo–German Naval Agreement, inspired in part by British fears over the growing size of the German Navy. The main feature of the agreement was that the German navy should not exceed one-third of the British navy. But under the agreement, German naval building expanded still further.

Sir Samuel Hoare, to meet French criticism, explained the British point of view on 11 July 1935, 'We saw a chance that might not recur of eliminating one of the causes that chiefly led to the embitterment before the Great War—the race of German naval armaments.'

British rearmament

The first real attempt at rearmament in Britain came in 1936, with the Navy the first priority, followed by the Army, then the RAF. In May 1937, Baldwin was replaced as Tory Prime Minister by Neville Chamberlain, who speeded up the rearmament process still more. But Winston Churchill was still not in the Government. In 1937, after Leslie Hore-Belisha had become Secretary of State for War, a mechanized division was at last formed, with Liddell-Hart playing a major part in the organization. Hore-Belisha told him: 'I owe everything to your advice.' But nine tanks out of ten were fit only for reconnaissance. Rearmament was moving at snail's pace. Britain's armed forces lagged far behind international events.

This inability of Britain and France to meet Hitler's threats of force with their own, and the fact that the Versailles Treaty had no provision for Allied action if Germany rearmed, forced Britain to rely heavily on the policy of 'appeasement', especially after Chamberlain had taken over from Baldwin.

Appeasement

Appeasement was based on the illusion that Hitler only wanted to reverse the wrongs which Germany felt had been done to her in 1919. Mussolini's aims were thought to be likewise limited to colonial objectives in north and east Africa. Chamberlain hoped that disputes could be settled by talks, and if the Italian and German claims were granted, peace in Europe would follow. Linked with this policy was an attempt to weaken the Rome–Berlin alliance.

It was this policy which was to motivate Chamberlain's actions at the time of Munich. Backed by Winston Churchill, still outside the Government, Anthony Eden (later Lord Avon) disagreed. Eden, the Foreign Secretary, believed the dictators should be checked by a common front of League members including Russia.

Anthony Eden (*right*) with Pierre Laval (the French Foreign Minister) in Paris during June 1935

Eden resigns

But Eden resigned in 1938, over Chamberlain's negotiations with Italy. In his resignation speech, Mr Eden said: '... I do not believe that we can make progress in European appeasement if we allow the impression to gain currency abroad that we yield to constant pressure ... I am certain in my own mind that progress depends above all on the temper of the nation, and that temper must find expression in a firm spirit. That spirit I am confident is there. Not to give voice to it is, I believe, fair neither to this country nor to the world (53).'

According to Churchill, 'From midnight till dawn I lay in my bed consumed by emotions of sorrow and fear. There seemed one strong young figure standing up against long, dismal, drawling tides of drift and surrender, of wrong measurements and feeble impulses ... Now he was gone. I watched the daylight slowly creep in through the windows, and saw before me in mental gaze the vision of Death (54).' Eden was replaced by Lord Halifax, a Chamberlain supporter. The Prime Minister now had a free hand for his appeasement policies in those fatal months of summer and autumn, 1938.

10 Munich

HITLER'S occupation of Austria, as well as strengthening his own *Czecho-slovakia* defences and weakening those of France, had strong repercussions in Czechoslovakia, his next target. Henlein's pro-Nazi party received increasing support. On 20 May the Czech army mobilized, in reply to reported German troop movements. Hitler ordered final preparations to be made for invasion. As with Austria, plans had been worked out long before.

In June 1937 the German Military Staff was told, 'The aim and *Hitler's policy* object of this surprise attack by the German armed forces should be to eliminate from the very beginning and for the duration of the war the threat from Czechoslovakia to the rear of the operations in the West ... (55).'

Hitler was later to say in a speech to the Reichstag in January 1939, 'I resolved to settle once and for all, and this time radically, the Sudeten–German question. On 28 May I ordered (i) that preparations should be made for military action against this State by 2 October; and (ii) the immense and accelerated expansion of our defensive front in the West ... (56).'

France was bound by treaty to rescue the Czechs. Britain would probably also be involved. Knowing this—and alarmed by the prospect—Chamberlain sent Lord Runciman to Prague in August, to persuade the Czechs to grant concessions which had been demanded by Henlein. Under pressure, the Czechs did so. Now, in the autumn, Henlein and Hitler demanded more. Chamberlain tried again.

89

Opposite A view of the mass parade at Nuremberg in 1937 where Hitler declared German policy towards Czechoslovakia

Chamberlain

On 15 September 1938, the British Prime Minister flew to Germany for talks with Hitler. On the following day, the French warned the Czech leader, Beneš, that France would only go to war if Britain did too. Meanwhile, Hitler was telling Chamberlain that he wanted nothing less than the cession of all land populated by Sudeten Germans.

Some views of Hitler

Neville Henderson, British Ambassador in Berlin, reported that Hitler did not want war, and that in his opinion Hitler's claims were morally justified. He wrote on 26 July: 'War would doubtless serve the purposes of all the Jews, Communists, and doctrinaires in the world for whom Nazism is anathema, but it would be a terrible risk today for Germany herself ... That this is not apparent to Hitler, I cannot believe. The Czechs are a pig-headed race and Beneš not the least pig-headed among them.'

Chamberlain shocked

Presented as he was with such inaccurate reports, Chamberlain's shock at his meeting with Hitler was even greater. Nevertheless, Chamberlain agreed to the Führer's demands, saying afterwards, 'On principle I had nothing to say against the separation of the Sudeten Germans from the rest of Czechoslovakia, provided that the practical difficulties could be overcome (57).'

He wrote, 'I got the impression that here was a man who could be relied upon when he had given his word.'

French and British Ministers hurriedly put their heads together in London, and on 19 September agreed to the cession of all predominantly German areas of Czechoslovakia—which would, incidentally, leave the rest of the country wide open to attack.

Selling out the Czechs

According to the official minutes of the conference, Lord Halifax said, 'Nothing was further from their thoughts than that the French Government should fail to honour their obligations to the Czechoslovak Government ... On the other hand we all knew—and he [Halifax] certainly thought their technical advisers would all agree with them in this—that whatever actions were taken by ourselves, by the French Government, or by the Soviet Government, at any given moment, it would be impossible to give effective protection to the Czechoslovak State. We might fight a war against German aggression, but at the peace conference which followed such a war he did not think that the statesmen concerned would redraft the present boundaries of Czechoslovakia (58).'

Litvinoff, the Russian representative at the League of Nations

Under pressure, Beneš accepted the plan on 21 September, the same day as the Russian representative at the League of Nations warned of the consequences of the agreement.

The Russian representative, Litvinov, also mentioned in the same *Russian fears* speech the attitude of other powers towards Russia, which was to ignore Soviet attempts to join in European negotiations. This policy by Britain and France was to play a part in pushing Russia into a pact with Germany a few months later (Chapter Ten):

'At the present time Czechoslovakia is suffering interference in its internal affairs at the hands of a neighbouring State ...

'Such an event as the disappearance of Austria passed unnoticed by the League of Nations. Realizing the significance of this event for the fate of the whole of Europe, and particularly of Czechoslovakia, the Soviet Government, immediately after the Anschluss, officially approached the other European Great Powers with a proposal for an immediate collective deliberation on the possible consequences of that event, in order to adopt collective preventive measures. To our regret, this proposal, which if carried out could

91

Left Neville Chamberlain leaves for Bad Godesberg and *right* with Sir Neville Henderson awaits Hitler's arrival there

have saved us from the alarm which all the world now feels for the fate of Czechoslovakia, did not receive its just appreciation ...(59).'

Chamberlain meets Hitler

On 22 September, Chamberlain reported back to Hitler at Godesberg. But in reply the German leader demanded occupation of the territory he claimed by 1 October, on which day he would invade unless he received Czech agreement by 28 September. He swept aside all Chamberlain's pleas for a more gradual takeover, and the German demands were formulated in the 'Godesberg Memorandum'.

The Czechs mobilized, complaining bitterly that Hitler's latest demands were 'absolutely and unconditionally unacceptable'. Even Britain and France feared war was now certain.

Halifax authorised the following press communiqué on 26 September: 'If a German attack is made upon Czechoslovakia ... France will be bound to come to her assistance, and Great Britain and Russia will certainly stand by France.' A diplomatic message,

Hitler and Chamberlain after their meeting in September 1938

saying the same as the communiqué, was given to Hitler.

Meanwhile Chamberlain explained his actions to an anxious House of Commons. The British Home Fleet was mobilized on 28 September.

Chamberlain had spoken to the nation on the radio the previous evening, 'How horrible, fantastic, incredible it is that we should be digging trenches and trying on gas-masks here because of a quarrel in a far-away country between people of whom we know nothing ... I would not hesitate to pay even a third visit to Germany if I thought it would do any good ... war is a fearful thing, and we must be very clear, before we embark on it, that it is really the great issues that are at stake.'

Chamberlain addresses the nation

The ultimatum thrown at the Czechs by Germany was fast running out. Desperately, Chamberlain appealed to Mussolini, and the Duce persuaded Hitler not to march for the moment. To the relief of Chamberlain, the Führer also agreed to a four-power conference

German ultimatum

93

between the Germans, British, Italians and French. The Czechs were not invited.

Chamberlain told the Commons: 'In reply to my message to Signor Mussolini, I was informed that instructions had been sent by the Duce ... that while Italy would fulfil completely her pledges to stand by Germany, yet, in view of the great importance of the request made by His Majesty's Government to Signor Mussolini, the latter hoped Herr Hitler would see his way to postpone action which the Chancellor had told Sir Horace Wilson was to be taken at 2 p.m. today [September 28] for at least 24 hours, so as to allow Signor Mussolini time to re-examine the situation and endeavour to find a peaceful settlement. In response, Herr Hitler has agreed.

'That is not all ... I have now been informed by Herr Hitler that he invites me to meet him at Munich tomorrow ... I need not say what my answer will be ... I am sure that the House will be ready to release me now to go and see what I can make of this last effort (60).'

Chamberlain at Munich
The conference met at Munich on 29 September, and signed the Munich Agreement the following day. Under the agreement, the Czechs were to start evacuating territory at once where, according to the Germans, more than fifty per cent of the population were German stock. The evacuation was to be finished in ten days time. The agreement was little different from the Godesberg Memorandum, except that the four powers were to supervise the transfer of territory, and guarantee the new Czech frontiers.

Here is the text of the main points: 'Agreement for the Cession by Czechoslovakia to Germany of Sudeten German Territory ...

'(1) The evacuation will begin on the 1 October.

'(2) The United Kingdom, France and Italy agree that the evacuation of the territory shall be completed by the 10 October ...

'(3) The conditions governing the evacuation will be laid down in detail by an international commission composed of representatives of Germany, the United Kingdom, France, Italy and Czechoslovakia.

'(4) The occupation by stages of the predominantly German territory by German troops will begin on the 1 October. The four territories marked on the attached map will be occupied by German troops (between 1 and 7 October). The remaining territory of preponderantly German character will be ascertained by the aforesaid

Duff Cooper resigned as First Lord of the Admiralty in protest at the Munich Agreement

international commission forthwith and be occupied by German troops by the 10 October.

'(5) The international commission referred to ... will determine the territories in which a plebiscite is to be held. These territories will be occupied by international bodies until the plebiscite has been completed ...

'(6) The final determination of the frontiers will be carried out by the international commission ...

'His Majesty's Government in the United Kingdom and the French Government have entered into the above agreement on the basis that they stand by the offer ... relating to an international guarantee of the new boundaries of the Czechoslovak State against unprovoked aggression ... (61).'

On 1 October, the Prime Minister's plane landed in England. Chamberlain stepped out, proclaiming he and Hitler had jointly renounced war in the settlement of national difficulties. 'This means peace in our time,' he said. Chamberlain believed it: many didn't.

'Peace in our time'

95

Duff Cooper, First Lord of the Admiralty, resigned on 2 October. He gave among his reasons: 'I besought my colleagues not to see this problem always in terms of Czechoslovakia, not to review it always from the difficult strategic position of that small country, but rather to say to themselves, "a moment may come when, owing to the invasion of Czechoslovakia, a European war will begin, and when that moment comes we must take part in that war, we cannot keep out of it, and there is no doubt upon which side we shall fight".

'Let the world know that, and it will give those who are prepared to disturb the peace reason to hold their hand ... The Prime Minister has believed in addressing Herr Hitler through the language of sweet reasonableness. I have believed that he was more open to the language of the mailed fist.'

Churchill declared, 'We have passed an awful milestone in our history, when the whole equilibrium of Europe has been deranged, and the terrible words have, for the time being, been pronounced against the Western Democracies: "Thou art weighed in the balance and found wanting".'

That same day, 30 September, the Czechs had to agree to all this. The Czech ministers 'wished to register their protest before the world against a decision in which they had no part'. Beneš resigned and fled to England.

Before leaving Hitler, Chamberlain had prepared this draft declaration which Hitler signed: 'We, the German Führer and Chancellor, and the British Prime Minister, have had a further meeting today, and are agreed in recognizing that the question of Anglo–German relations is of the first importance for the two countries and for Europe.

'We regard the Agreement signed last night, and the Anglo–German Naval Agreements, as symbolic of the desire of our two peoples never to go to war with one another again.

'We are resolved that the method of consultation shall be the method adopted to deal with any other questions that may concern our two countries, and we are determined to continue our efforts to remove possible sources of difference, and thus to contribute to assure the peace of Europe (62).'

Yet whatever the strength of Chamberlain's beliefs, and those of the many who supported him, Britain embarked on a rearmament programme such as she had never before attempted in time of peace. The last brittle pretensions of peace were snapping.

Hitler said at Saarbrucken on 9 October: 'The statesmen who are opposed to us wish for peace ... but they govern in countries whose domestic organization makes it possible that at any time they may lose their position to make way for others who are not anxious for peace. And those others are there. *Hitler justifies himself*

'It only needs that in England instead of Chamberlain, Mr. Duff Cooper or Mr. Eden or Mr. Churchill should come to power, and then we know quite well that it would be the aim of these men immediately to begin a new World War ...

'I have therefore decided ... to continue the construction of our fortifications in the West with increased energy ... It would be a good thing if in Great Britain people would gradually drop certain airs which they have inherited from the Versailles epoch.

'We cannot tolerate any longer the tutelage of governesses. Inquiries of British politicians concerning the fate of Germans within the frontiers of the Reich, or of others belonging to the Reich, are not in place (63).'

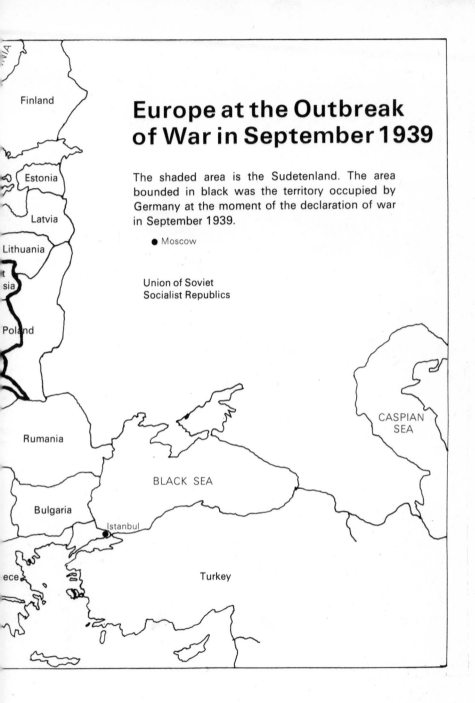

Europe at the Outbreak of War in September 1939

The shaded area is the Sudetenland. The area bounded in black was the territory occupied by Germany at the moment of the declaration of war in September 1939.

● Moscow

Union of Soviet
Socialist Republics

Finland

Estonia

Latvia

Lithuania

t
sia

Poland

Rumania

BLACK SEA

Bulgaria

Istanbul

CASPIAN
SEA

ece

Turkey

99

11 Poland—and War

HITLER was dissatisfied with the Munich Agreement. On 15 March 1939, he extended his rule over the entire country and handed out spoils to Hungary and Poland. The Führer arrived in Prague. The Slovaks were allowed to declare their own independence, in the German shadow.

According to Chamberlain, the British guarantee to protect the Czech borders had been invalidated by this Slovak breakaway. He told the Commons on 15 March, 'The effect of this declaration put an end by internal disruption to the State whose frontiers we had proposed to guarantee, and His Majesty's Government cannot accordingly hold themselves bound by this obligation'. *Let-out for Britain*

Hitler was now almost ready to turn to Poland. But first he secured himself by a full military alliance with Italy through the so-called 'Pact of Steel' signed on 22 May. Mussolini was now bound to come to Hitler's aid if he 'became involved in warlike complications'. *Pact of Steel*

Chamberlain had abruptly changed his attitude. In a speech at Birmingham on 17 March he declared: 'We are told that this seizure of territory (in Czechoslovakia) has been necessitated by disturbances in Czechoslovakia … If there were disorders, were they not fomented from without? … Is this the last attack upon a small State, or is it to be followed by another? Is this in fact a step in the direction of an attempt to dominate the world by force?' *Chamberlain drops appeasement*

The speech was also notable for the description Chamberlain gave of his 'appeasement' policy—a policy which was now being discarded. Let us hear his speech again: '… Public opinion in the world has received a sharper shock than has ever yet been admini-

Opposite Hitler and his Nazis; front, left to right: Gestapo chief Himmler, Minister of the Interior Frick, General von Epp, Goering. Back, left to right: Governor of Saxony Nutschmann, Goebbels, Education Minister Rust

stered to it, even by the present regime in Germany. What may be the ultimate effects of this profound disturbance on men's minds cannot yet be foretold, but I am sure that it must be far-reaching in its results upon the future ...'

Chamberlain went on, 'It has been suggested that this occupation of Czecho-Slovakia was the direct consequence of the visit which I paid to Germany last autumn ...

'I went there first and foremost because, in what appeared to be an almost desperate situation, that seemed to me to offer the only chance of averting a European war. And I might remind you that, when it was first announced that I was going, not a voice was raised in criticism ...'

He added, 'I have never denied that the terms which I was able to secure at Munich were not those that I myself would have desired. But, as I explained then, I had to deal with no new problem. This was something that had existed ever since the Treaty of Versailles— a problem that ought to have been solved long ago if only the statesmen of the last 20 years had taken broader and more enlightened views of their duty ...

'The first and the most immediate object of my visit was achieved. The peace of Europe was saved.'

Plaintively, he continued, 'Really I have no need to defend my visits to Germany last autumn, for what was the alternative? Nothing that we could have done, nothing that France could have done ... could possibly have saved Czecho-Slovakia from invasion and destruction ...

'But I had another purpose ... That was to further the policy ... sometimes called European appeasement ... If that policy were to succeed, it was essential that no Power should seek to obtain a general domination of Europe ... I felt that ... by the exercise of mutual goodwill and understanding of what were the limits of the desires of others, it should be possible to resolve all differences by discussion and without armed conflict.'

Chamberlain spoke of what Hitler had assured him: '[Herr Hitler] repeated what he had already said at Berchtesgaden— namely, that this was the last of his territorial ambitions in Europe, and that he had no wish to include in the Reich people of other races than German ...

'Germany, under her present regime, has sprung a series of unpleasant surprises upon the world. The Rhineland, the Austrian
"Anschluss", the severance of Sudetenland—all these things
shocked and affronted public opinion throughout the world.

'Unpleasant
surprises'

'Yet, however much we might take exception to the methods
which were adopted in each of those cases, there was something to
be said, whether on account of racial affinity or of just claims too
long resisted—there was something to be said for the necessity of a
change in the existing situation.'

Wearily, he summed up, 'But the events which have taken place
this week in complete disregard of the principles laid down by the
German Government itself seem to fall into a different category ...
(64)'

On 31 March Chamberlain announced to the Commons that
Britain was signing a military alliance with Poland.

'I may add that the French Government have authorized me to
make it plain that they stand in the same position in this matter
as do His Majesty's Government.'

On 27 April, military conscription was introduced in Britain. The
same day, Germany denounced the naval agreement with Britain,
and the following day denounced the German–Polish agreement.

British
conscription

This was how Germany denounced the agreement with Britain:
'When in the year 1935 the German Government made the British
Government the offer to bring the strength of the German fleet to a
fixed proportion of the strength of the naval forces of the British
Empire by means of a treaty, it did so on the basis of the firm convic-
tion that for all time the recurrence of a warlike conflict between
Germany and Great Britain was excluded ...

Germany
denounces
Agreement
with Britain

'The German Government has always adhered to this wish and
still today is inspired by it. It is conscious of having acted accordingly in its policy and of having in no case intervened in the sphere
of English interests or of having in any way encroached on these
interests. On the other hand it must to its regret take note of the fact
that the British Government of late is departing more and more from
the course of an analogous policy towards Germany ... The British
Government thus regards war by England against Germany no
longer as an impossibility, but on the contrary as a capital problem
of English foreign policy ...(65)'

103

Beck, the Polish leader, arrives in London during April 1939 for talks on
the Polish crisis

*German–
Polish Pact
torn up*

The excuse used by Hitler for scrapping his pact with Poland,
signed in 1934, was the Anglo–Polish guarantee. Following Chamberlain's speech of 31 March, the Polish leader—Beck—had visited
London. An Anglo–Polish communiqué stated, 'The conversations
with M. Beck have covered a wide field and shown that the two
Governments are in complete agreement upon certain general
principles.

'It was agreed that the two countries were prepared to enter into
an agreement of a permanent and reciprocal character to replace the
present temporary and unilateral assurance given by His Majesty's
Government to the Polish Government ...(66)'

Hitler told the Reichstag on 28 April that this Anglo–Polish
Guarantee 'would in certain circumstances compel Poland to
take military action against Germany in the event of a conflict
between Germany and any other Power, in which England in her
turn would be involved ...(67)'

But once again, Hitler had already carefully prepared his take-

over plans. On 24 October, Ribbentrop had proposed to the Polish *Lighting the*
Ambassador in Berlin that the Free City of Danzig should be *fuse*
handed back to Germany. The Poles had refused. Late in January,
1939, Ribbentrop again tried to persuade the Poles to hand over the
city. And on 27 March a Nazi press campaign was launched, accusing the Poles of atrocious behaviour towards their German minority. Danzig and this alleged behaviour were to be the pretexts for
the invasion.

Hitler told a Chiefs of Staff meeting on 23 May, 'Poland will
always be on the side of our adversaries ... Poland has always had
the secret intention of exploiting every opportunity to do us harm.
Danzig is not the subject of the dispute at all. It is a question of
expanding our living space in the East and of securing our food
supplies. There is therefore no question of sparing Poland, and we
are left with the decision to attack Poland at the first suitable opportunity. We cannot expect a repetition of the Czech affair. There will
be war ... I doubt the possibility of a peaceful settlement with
England. We must prepare ourselves for the conflict.'

Yet on 3 August, the British Minister for Coordination of
Defence, Sir Thomas Inskip, said, 'War today is not only not inevitable, but is unlikely. The Government have good reason for
saying that.'

Nevertheless, on 22 August, Britain warned Germany about her *Chamberlain*
action with regard to Poland. Chamberlain wrote to Hitler, mak- *writes to Hitler*
ing British policy clear beyond a shadow of a doubt:

'Your Excellency ... apparently the announcement of a German–
Soviet Agreement is taken in some quarters in Berlin to indicate that
intervention by Great Britain on behalf of Poland is no longer a
contingency that need be reckoned with ...

'It has been alleged that, if His Majesty's Government had made
their position more clear in 1914, the great catastrophe would have
been avoided. Whether or not there is any force in that allegation,
His Majesty's Government are resolved that on this occasion there
shall be no such tragic misunderstanding.

'If the case should arise, they are resolved, and prepared, to
employ without delay all the forces at their command, and it is
impossible to foresee the end of hostilities once engaged ...(68)'

There was mounting apprehension over a possible German–

The signing of the ominous Nazi-Soviet Pact in 1939

Russo–
German
Pact

Russian agreement, which could perhaps include tearing apart Poland between themselves. On the very next day, 23 August, the Russo–German Pact was signed.

Agreement between Communist Russia and Nazi Germany—the two outcasts of Europe—shocked the Western diplomatic world. According to Article I of the Non-Aggression Treaty between the two countries, 'Both High Contracting Parties [agree] to desist from any act of violence, any aggressive action, and any attack on each other, either individually or jointly with other powers.'

Article IV added, 'Neither of the two High Contracting Parties shall participate in any grouping of powers whatsoever that is directly or indirectly aimed at the other party ...'

Yet Stalin and Hitler personally loathed each other. Both had made the defeat of the other's doctrines a major aim of their international policies. There is plentiful evidence that Stalin was pushed into this union by the reluctance of the non-Nazi powers to negotiate with him. Russia needed protection as much as anyone and Britain and France had time and again refused the kind of not unreasonable alliance which Stalin wanted.

Russia courts
Britain

Russia had wanted a precise alliance for mutual assistance. The British, who had worked hard to keep Russia isolated, would only offer a promise of aid to Russia under strict conditions. Negotiations between Britain and Russia took place from late spring 1939 throughout summer. On 14 April Britain proposed a distinctly one-sided bargain, asking that if a Russian neighbour were attacked: 'the assistance of the Soviet Government would be available, if desired, and would be afforded in such a manner as would be found most convenient.'

On 18 April this was rejected by Russia, who said there should be a full-scale alliance. Britain replied: 'His Majesty's Government might be drawn into a war not for the preservation of the independence of a minor European state but for the support of the Soviet Union against Germany.'

On 9 May, Britain tried again. In view of the British guarantees to Poland and Rumania, 'the Soviet Government would undertake that in the event of Great Britain and France being involved in hostilities in fulfilment of these obligations the assistance of the Soviet Government would be immediately available, if desired, and would be afforded in such a manner and on such terms as might be agreed (69).'

Molotov, now Foreign Affairs Commissar, not surprisingly, turned this down. And so talks continued through until August.

To Stalin, the British offers were not enough. To buy time, therefore, he turned now to Hitler. He gained something else, too. Under secret terms of the Treaty, Hitler and Stalin agreed to divide Poland between them.

A German attack on Poland now seemed imminent. Hitler had in fact decided to time his invasion for late August, but his move was delayed by the news that Mussolini was not quite ready, and by the announcement of the signature of the formal Anglo–Polish Agreement.

Anglo–Polish Agreement

These were the terms of this agreement:

'(1) Should one of the Contracting Parties become engaged in hostilities with a European Power in consequence of aggression by the latter against that Contracting Party, the other Contracting Party will at once give the Contracting Party engaged in hostilities all the support and assistance in its power.

'(2) The provisions of Article 1 will also apply in the event of any action by a European Power which clearly threatened, directly or indirectly, the independence of one of the Contracting Parties, and was of such a nature that the Party in question considered it vital to resist it with armed forces (70).'

By 31 August it was clear to Hitler all chance of negotiation had gone, and he issued his 'Directive Number 1 for the Conduct of War'.

The date of attack would be 1 September:

'(1) Now that all the political possibilities of disposing by peaceful means of a situation on the Eastern frontier which is intolerable for Germany are exhausted, I have determined on a solution by force.

Hitler's plan of attack

'(2) The attack on Poland is to be carried out in accordance with the preparation made for "Fall Weiss" ... Allotments of tasks and the operational targets remain unchanged. The date of attack— 1 September 1939. Time of attack—04·45.

'(3) In the West it is important that the responsibility for the opening of hostilities should rest unequivocally with England and France. At first purely local action should be taken against insignificant frontier violations (71).'

So in the early hours of 1 September 1939, the Germans invaded Poland. There was no declaration of war. The pretext was an attack, made by Germans in stolen Polish uniforms, on Gleiwitz radio station. Britain sent an ultimatum to Germany demanding that she agree to withdraw forces from Polish soil.

The British Ultimatum of 1 September was followed by this telegram from the British Foreign Secretary to the British Ambassador at Berlin, 3 September 1939, 5 a.m.:

'Please seek interview with Minister for Foreign Affairs at 9 a.m. today, Sunday, or, if he cannot see you then, arrange to convey at that time to representative of German Government the following communication:

"In the communication [of] 1 September I informed you, on the instructions of His Majesty's Principal Secretary of State for Foreign Affairs, that, unless the German Government were prepared to give His Majesty's Government in the United Kingdom satisfactory assurances that the German Government had suspended all aggressive action against Poland and were prepared promptly to withdraw their forces from Polish Territory, His Majesty's Government in the United Kingdom would, without hesitation, fulfil their obligations to Poland.

"Although this communication was made more than twenty four hours ago, no reply has been received but German attacks upon Poland have been continued and intensified. I have accordingly the honour to inform you that, unless not later than 11 a.m., British Summer Time, today 3 September, satisfactory assurances to the above effect have been given by the German Government and have reached his Majesty's Government in London, a state of war will exist between the two countries from that hour."'

The telegram to the British Ambassador continued:

'If the assurance referred to in the above communication is received, you should inform me by any means at your disposal before 11 am today 3 September. If no such assurance is received here by 11 am, we shall inform the German representative that a state of war exists as from that hour (72).'

The same evening, Chamberlain solemnly addressed the Commons: 'We shall stand at the bar of history knowing that the responsibility for this terrible catastrophe lies on the shoulders of one man—the German Chancellor, who has not hesitated to plunge the world into misery in order to serve his own senseless ambitions.'

Meanwhile that 'one man' was haranguing the Reichstag: 'I am asking of no German man more than I myself was ready throughout four years at any time to do. There will be no hardships for Germans to which I myself will not submit. My whole life henceforth belongs more than ever to my people. I am from now on just first soldier of the German Reich.' Hitler refused to accept the British demands. This was his reply at 11.20 a.m., 3 September: *Hitler replies*

'The German Government have received the British Government's ultimatum of the 3 September, 1939. They have the honour to reply as follows:

'(1) The German Government and the German people refuse to receive, accept, let alone fulfil, demands in the nature of ultimata made by the British Government.

'(2) On our eastern frontier there has for many months already reigned a condition of war. Since the time when the Versailles Treaty first tore Germany to pieces, all and every peaceful settlement was refused to all German Governments. The National Socialist Government also had since the year 1933 tried again and again to

109

remove by peaceful negotiations the worst rapes and breaches of justice of this treaty.

Hitler accuses 'The British Government have been among those who, by their intransigent attitude, took the chief part in frustrating every practical revision. Without the intervention of the British Government— of this the German Government and German people are fully conscious—a reasonable solution doing justice to both sides would certainly have been found between Germany and Poland ...

'(3) The British Government have—an occurrence unique in history—given the Polish State full powers for all actions against Germany which that State might conceivably intend to undertake ... The Free City of Danzig was, in violation of all legal provisions, first threatened with destruction economically and by measures of customs policy, and was finally subjected to a military blockade and its communications strangled ...

'All these happenings were known in every detail to the British Government [which] therefore, bear the responsibility for all the unhappiness and misery which have now overtaken and are about to overtake many peoples.

'(4) After all efforts at finding and concluding a peaceful solution had been rendered impossible by the intransigence of the Polish Government covered as they were by England, after the conditions resembling civil war, which had existed already for months at the eastern frontier of the Reich, had gradually developed into open attacks on German territory, without the British Government raising any objections, the German Government determined to put an end to this continual threat ...

'(5) The German Government, therefore, reject the attempt to force Germany, by means of a demand having the character of an ultimatum, to recall its forces which are lined up for the defence of the Reich, and thereby to accept the old unrest and the old injustice.

'The threat that, failing this, they will fight Germany in the war, corresponds to the intention proclaimed for years past by numerous British politicians ...

'The intention ... of carrying the destruction of the German people even further than was done through the Versailles Treaty is taken note of by us, and we shall therefore answer any aggressive action on the part of England with the same weapon and in the same form (73).'

The British ultimatum had expired twenty minutes earlier, 11 a.m. British Summer Time. On 3 September, therefore, Britain and France declared war on Germany.

That fateful day, Chamberlain solemnly addressed the British nation on the radio: 'I am speaking to you from the Cabinet Room at 10 Downing Street. This morning the British Ambassador in Berlin handed the German Government a final Note stating that unless we heard from them by 11 o'clock that they were prepared at once to withdraw their troops from Poland a state of war would exist between us. I have to tell you now that no such undertaking has been received, and that consequently this country is at war with Germany ...

'Up to the very last it would have been quite possible to have arranged a peaceful and honourable settlement between Germany and Poland. But Hitler would not have it. He had evidently made up his mind to attack Poland whatever happened; and although he now says he put forward reasonable proposals which were rejected by the Poles, that is not a true statement.

'The proposals were never shown to the Poles nor to us; and though they were announced in the German broadcast on Thursday night, Hitler did not wait to hear comments on them, but ordered his troops to cross the Polish frontier next morning.

'His action shows convincingly that there is no chance of expecting that this man will ever give up his practice of using force to gain his will. He can only be stopped by force and we and France are today, in fulfilment of our obligations, going to the aid of Poland (74).'

Churchill wrote, 'Once again we must fight for life and honour against all the might and fury of the valiant, disciplined, and ruthless German race. Once again! So be it!'

Chamberlain speaks to Britain

12 Japan

JAPAN not only felt that diplomatically and historically she ought to be the centre of power in Asia, but by the mid-1930s there was an economic reason too. Worldwide depression had reduced foreign demand for her exports, and previous markets had built tariff barriers. Many Japanese now believed they should acquire more markets of their own—through territorial acquisition.

Japanese economy

Chinese nationalism was at this time becoming more insistent, and Communism was threatening from the north. The Japanese therefore decided to extend their influence, by diplomacy and military action. The Hirota Cabinet, in a statement on 11 August 1936, stated: '... the fundamental national policy to be established by the Empire is to secure the position of the Empire on the East Asia Continent by dint of diplomatic policy and national defense, mutually dependent on each other, as well as to advance and develop the Empire toward the South Seas (75).'

The Japanese believed, with good reason, that America had neither the power to protect China or European possessions in Asia, nor the willingness—at that stage—to become involved.

Anti-Comintern Pact

What followed should have surprised no one. In November 1936, the 'Anti-Comintern Pact' was signed between Germany and Japan. It declared, 'The Government of the German Reich and the Imperial Japanese Government: In recognition of the fact that the aim of the Communist International, called "Comintern", is the disintegration of, and the commission of violence against, existing States with all means at its command ... Desiring to cooperate for defence against Communist disintegration, have agreed as follows:

'(1) The high contracting States agree mutually to keep one

113

Opposite: above Hitler receiving a Japanese naval delegation in 1934. *Below left* General Hideki Tojo, the militant Japanese premier who brought his country into the war. *Right* Prince Fumimaro Konoye, Prime Minister of Japan before the outbreak of war

another informed concerning counter-measures and to carry out the latter in close collaboration.

'(2) The high contracting States will jointly invite third States whose internal peace is menaced by the disintegrating work of the Communist International to adopt defensive measures in the spirit of the present agreement or to participate in the present agreement ...(76)'

Japan attacks China

A few months later, in July 1937 Japan invaded China. The Nine-Power Treaty, signed by Japan on 6 February 1922, was violated. According to Article 1, 'The Contracting Powers, other than China, agree: (i) to respect the sovereignty, the independence, and the territorial and administrative integrity of China ...'

American difficulty

America was in a difficult position. What was she to do? If action were taken against Japan, or even mediation attempted as China requested, there would be more support inside Japan for the war party. America could find herself in a conflict she could not afford.

Cordell Hull, Secretary of State, said on 17 August that America was caught between two views: 'One is the view of extreme internationalism, which rests upon the idea of political commitments. We keep entirely away from that in our thoughts and views and policies, just as we seek, on the other hand, to keep entirely away from the extreme nationalists who would tell all Americans they must stay here at home.'

The League of Nations duly declared Japan an aggressor. But retaliation against Japan was not attempted. Instead, a conference was called at Brussels, and, as the American President said on the radio on 12 October, 'The purpose of this conference will be to seek by agreement a solution of the present situation in China. In efforts to find that solution, it is our purpose to cooperate with the other signatories of the Treaty, including China and Japan.'

Britain was fully occupied in Europe. And by November it was obvious to all that the conference was a failure. Meanwhile, the Japanese marched on. On 10 February the island of Hainan, between Hong Kong and Singapore, was occupied. In March 1938, sovereignty was claimed over coral islands in the Spratly group.

Oil for Japan

The American Administration were seriously considering stopping the supply of US oil and scrap iron to Japan, the raw materials of war on which Japan heavily depended. Admiral Yonai, the

President Roosevelt of the United States (*right*) and his Secretary of State
Cordell Hull (*left*)

Japanese Prime Minister, warned his countrymen on 23 March 1940: 'The question of a general embargo is a serious one both for the country imposing the embargo and the country upon which it is imposed. If one false step is taken, danger lies ahead for both countries.' It was the time of the 'phoney' war in Europe. But any phoniness was abruptly shattered on 10 May, with German attacks on Holland, Belgium and France.

World reactions

In 1922, America, Britain, France and Japan had resolved 'to respect the rights of the Netherlands in relation to their insular possessions in the region of the Pacific Ocean'. Now, with Holland in chaos, America and Britain were apprehensive over how Japan would react towards the Dutch East Indies. Churchill, on 15 May, urged President Roosevelt to send warships to Singapore. But the President refused. America did not want to increase the Far East tension, nor did she have enough forces for both the Pacific and for the Atlantic if they were needed.

On 18 June Japan demanded that the Pétain Government in France should allow a Japanese 'military mission' to operate in

Indo-China. Under pressure, France gave way two days later. In the same month, Japan threatened Britain with war unless British troops were shipped out of Shanghai and the border between Hong Kong and China were closed. Japan planned to cut China off from the outside world.

US National Defense Act   America retaliated with the National Defense Act in May, which permitted the President to keep all products at home that might be needed for defence—including oil. Section VI of the Act declared,

'Whenever the President determines that it is necessary in the interest of national defense to prohibit or curtail the exportation of any military equipment or munitions, or component parts thereof, or machinery, tools, or materials or supplies necessary for the manufacture, servicing or operation thereof, he may by proclamation prohibit or curtail such exportation, except under such rules or regulations as he shall prescribe ...(77)'

Japanese policy   In Tokyo, the Japanese disagreed as to how far and fast their policy should move. Many were still reluctant to take on the United States. The Army however, wanting more action, caused the resignation of Yonai, and Prince Konoye once again became Prime Minister.

On 27 July the Japanese Cabinet stated its policy: 'to maintain a firm attitude toward America on the one hand ... to take stronger measures against French Indo-China, Hong Kong and foreign concessions in China looking to the prevention of aid to the Chiang regime ... To practise more vigorous diplomacy towards the Netherlands East Indies, in order to acquire vital materials ...(78)'

On 6 August, Japan demanded that France should let Japanese troops move across Tonkin province, Indo-China, bordering on China. The French reluctantly agreed on 29 August. Next month the Japanese completely overran the province.

A Japanese policy document was formulated on 4 September, stating: 'The sphere to be envisaged in the course of negotiations with Germany and Italy as Japan's Sphere of Living for the construction of a Greater East Asia New Order will comprise: The former German Islands under mandate, French Indo-China and Pacific Islands, Thailand, British Malaya, British Borneo, Dutch East Indies, Burma, Australia, New Zealand, India, *etc.*, with Japan, Manchuria and China as the backbone (79).'

At the same time, Japan increased her demands for oil from the Indies. President Roosevelt now ordered complete control of all exports of iron and steel scrap to Japan; but oil was still left unrestricted.

The Tripartite Pact signed between Japan, Germany and Italy *Tripartite Pact* on 27 September made an obvious reference to America: 'we all further undertake to assist one another with all political, economic and military means when one of the three Contracting Parties is attacked by a power at present not involved in the European War or in the Sino–Japanese conflict.'

Britain was very anxious at this time to know of America's intentions, and on 7 February 1941 the British Embassy told the US State Department, 'Evidence is accumulating that the Japanese may already have decided to push on southward even if this means war (80).'

Britain and America did in fact move closer, for example the Joint Staff Conferences had started in Washington on 29 January. But America still refused to enter the European war, or to promise help if Singapore or the Indies were attacked by Japan.

The Japanese militarists received support from Nazi Germany. *Hitler and Japan* According to a Naval Staff report for Hitler, early in January 1941, 'it is in our interest to encourage Japan to take any initiative she considers within her power in the Far Eastern area, as this would be most likely to keep American forces from the European theatre in addition to weakening and tying down British forces.'

A few weeks later the Führer, planning to attack Russia ('Operation Barbarossa') thought Japan could be extremely useful to him. A Military Directive on 5 March stated, 'It must be the aim of the collaboration based on the Three Power Pact to induce Japan as soon as possible to take active measures in the Far East ... The seizure of Singapore ... would mean a decisive success for the entire conduct of war of the Three Powers. In addition attacks on other systems of bases of British naval power—extending to those of American naval power only if entry of the United States into the war cannot be prevented—will result in the weakening of the enemy's system of power in that region (81).'

At last, on 20 June, America announced an embargo on oil ex- *Konoye's policy* ports to eastern ports. Some oil was still finding its way to Japan, but in Tokyo the latest restriction deepened the split between those who wanted to help Germany attack Russia, and those—including Konoye—who wanted to open talks with America. A compromise was reached on 2 July which let Konoye continue talks with America, but which laid down that Japan should secure control over all Indo–China. This was how the Japanese policy was drawn up:

'(1) *Policy.* The Imperial Government is determined to follow a policy which will result in the establishment of the Greater East Asia Co-Prosperity Sphere and world peace, no matter what international developments take place ...

'(2) *Summary.* In order to guarantee national security and preservation, the Imperial Government will continue all necessary diplomatic negotiations ... In case the diplomatic negotiations break down, preparations for a war with England and America will also be carried forward. First of all, the plans which have been laid with reference to French Indo–China and Thailand will be prosecuted ...

'(3) Our attitude with reference to the German–Soviet War will be based on the spirit of the Tri-Partite Pact. However, we will not enter the conflict for some time ... In case the German–Soviet War should develop to our advantage, we will make use of our military strength, settle the Soviet question and guarantee the safety of our northern borders ...

'(6) We will immediately turn our attention to placing the nation on a war basis ...(82)'

So the Japanese entry into Indo–China started. Plans were made for moves against Malaya, the East Indies, Borneo, and the Philippines.

The Navy began to practise for attacks on Pearl Harbour.

On 1 August, America made up her mind. She finally decided there should be a complete oil embargo. Japan tried to bargain, offering to withdraw from Indo–China after the settlement of the China war—if normal US trade were resumed.

Roosevelt   Before doing anything, Roosevelt met Churchill, and it was agreed that Japan should be seriously warned. The American President told the Japanese Ambassador, Nomura, '... if the Japanese Government takes any further steps in pursuance of a policy or programme of military domination by force or threat of force of neighbouring countries, the Government of the United States will be compelled to take immediately any and all steps which it may deem necessary toward safeguarding the legitimate rights and interests of the United States (83).'

Believing that Britain and America would soon join hands in their *Japanese* defences in the Far East, the Japanese War Minister, Tojo, and *differences* senior army commanders demanded that talks should finish and war begin as soon as the Japanese forces were in position and before America and Britain were ready. Konoye strongly disagreed. Once more there was a compromise, and Konoye was given more time. But the army went on with its preparations for swift control of Java, Sumatra, Borneo and Malaya, in order to secure oil, rubber, iron ore and other essentials.

Diplomatic talks with America became deadlocked. Terms offered by Tokyo would have let Japan control China and retain the chance of more expansion later. Terms offered by Washington would have meant Japan accepting defeat in China. Eventually, on 16 October, Konoye was replaced by the militant Tojo, who now combined the position of War Minister with that of Prime Minister.

General Sugiyama, the Chief of General Staff, told the Liaison Conference on 23 October that a decision on peace or war should be made soon. Military plans and training were almost complete. But it was decided one last attempt should be made at diplomacy. Talks began with the United States on 10 November. Japan began by restating previous terms, but these were rejected by America over the issue of retention of control of China. Then Nomura, the Japanese Ambassador, presented a second—and final—set of proposals.

These amounted to putting back the clock as it was before July, before Japan had moved into southern Indo–China and the American embargo had been imposed. For a while, the Americans thought this could be a means to allow more time. But the proposals included one fatal paragraph, which was completely unacceptable:

'(5) The Government of the United States undertakes to refrain from such measures and actions as will be prejudicial to the endeavours for the restoration of general peace between Japan and China (84).'

According to Hull, US Secretary of State, acceptance would mean condoning Japan's past aggressions. The final proposals were therefore thrown out, and on 7 December 1941 the first Japanese troop landings were made at Kotabharu, British Malaya.

One and a half hours later the American Pacific fleet was bombed at Pearl Harbour. War had begun.

Britain declared war in the following, courteous fashion in this letter to the Japanese Ambassador in London:

Foreign Office, December 8.

'*Sir*, On the evening of December 7th His Majesty's Government in the United Kingdom learned that Japanese forces without previous warning either in the form of a declaration of war or of an ultimatum with a conditional declaration of war had attempted a landing on the coast of Malaya and bombed Singapore and Hong Kong.

'In view of these wanton acts of unprovoked aggression committed in flagrant violation of International Law and particularly of Article 1 of the Third Hague Convention relative to the opening of hostilities, to which both Japan and the United Kingdom are parties, His Majesty's Ambassador at Tokyo has been instructed to inform the Imperial Japanese Government in the name of His Majesty's Government in the United Kingdom that a state of war exists between our two countries.

'I have the honour to be, with high consideration,

Sir,

Your obedient servant,
Winston S. Churchill.'

Opposite The Japanese air attack on the American navy at Pearl Harbour on 8th December, 1941

Epilogue

Complex era FEW WARS, if any, have a single origin. Outbreak of conflict comes from a clash of various causes. This was certainly true of the First World War, yet it was overlooked by the peacemakers of 1919. Exhausted, physically and mentally, by four years of slaughter, four years of hysterically 'hating the Hun', they picked on one reason for it all: Germany. And this was written into the peace treaty, and therefore into the peace.

The peacemaking was a longer struggle than the war itself, and the effects of the work at Versailles were to have repercussions down the decades. German aggression had been just one of the reasons for the war. Later politicians, not only in Germany, realized this. In Germany, grievance festered.

Moreover, the exhausted peacemakers hoped to create a better, safer world, a world of democracies. But their attempts to do so made the flimsy balance of power in Europe even more fragile. Too many pretexts were left around for future quarrels: Danzig, the Saar, Teschen.

Weak democracies The democracies themselves largely failed and, in the insecurity of the failures, dictators seized their chances: in Russia, Italy, and above all, in Germany. Stalin, Mussolini, and Hitler—and Franco in Spain—used violent methods and private armies to climb to power, and used them to consolidate that power: Stalin with his 1936 purges, Mussolini with his war against Abyssinia to create unity at home, Hitler with his 'Night of the Long Knives' and his massacre of the Jews.

In this new world of renewed violence in public life, the old democracies were unprepared not only to protect others, but also themselves. More opportunities were offered to the dictators, and they seized them, banding together in that fateful year of 1939 to explode even more of a world-wide conflict than that which had erupted a quarter of a century before.

Notes on Sources

(1) *Congressional Record*, Volume *lvi* (1918)

(2) Harold Nicolson, *Peacemaking 1919* (Methuen, 1964)

(3) *The Treaty of Peace between the Allied and Associated Powers and Germany* (H.M.S.O., 1919)

(4) British and Foreign State Papers, Volume *cxii* (1919)

(5) F.A. Golder, *Documents of Russian History, 1914–1917* (The Century Press, 1927)

(6) *International Conciliation* (1918)

(7) W.H. Chamberlain, *The Russian Revolution 1917–1921* (Macmillan, 1935)

(8) Mussolini, *My Autobiography* (Hutchinson, 1939)

(9) Rappard, *Source Book of European Government* (New York, 1937)

(10) *Ibid*

(11) *Treaty of Peace between the Allied and Associated Powers and Germany* (H.M.S.O., 1919, Cmd. 153)

(12) Kertesz, *Documents in the Political History of the European Continent, 1815–1939* (Oxford, 1968)

(13) *Ibid*

(14) Rappard, *Source Book on European Government*

(15) E. B. Wheaton, *Prelude to Calamity* (Gollancz, 1969)

(16) *International Conciliation* (1924)

(17) *British and Foreign State Papers*, Volume *cxviii* (1923)

(18) *League of Nations Treaty Series* (1926–7)

(19) *Ibid*

(20) *Ibid*

(21) Kertesz, *Documents in the Political History of the European Continent, 1815–1939*

(22) Goebbels, *Angriff* (May, 1928)

(23) Wheaton, *Prelude to Calamity*

(24) *Ibid*

(25) *British and Foreign State Papers*, Volume *cxxxvi* (1933)

(26) *Ibid*

(27) Wheaton, *Prelude to Calamity*

(28) *Documents on International Affairs 1933* (Oxford)

(29) Baynes, *Hitler's Speeches*

(30) Spengler, *Politische Pflichten der deutschen Jugend*

(31) Spengler, *Der Mensch und die Technik*

(32) Spengler, *Jahre der Entscheidung*

(33) Werth, *France in Ferment*

(34) Churchill, *The Gathering Storm*

(35) *League of Nations Journal: 1935* (Oxford)

(36) *British and Foreign State*

Papers, Volume *cxl* (1936)
(37) Churchill, *The Gathering Storm*
(38) Kertesz, *Documents in the Political History of the European Continent, 1815–1939*
(39) *League of Nations Journal* (1937)
(40) A. J. P. Taylor, *Europe: Grandeur and Decline* (Penguin, 1967)
(41) Churchill, *The Gathering Storm*
(42) Baynes, *Hitler's Speeches*
(43) *Documents on International Affairs*
(44) *League of Nations Journal* (1935)
(45) Churchill, *The Gathering Storm*
(46) *Documents on International Affairs* (Oxford, 1935)
(47) Chapman, *Why France Collapsed*
(48) Churchill, *The Gathering Storm*
(49) Fuller, *On Future Warfare*
(50) Churchill, *The Gathering Storm*
(51) *Ibid*
(52) *Ibid*
(53) *Ibid*
(54) *Ibid*
(55) *Nuremberg Documents*, II
(56) *Hitler's Speeches*, II
(57) *Documents on British Foreign Policy*
(58) *Documents on British Foreign Policy, 1919–39*, (third series, 1938)
(59) *League of Nations Journal* (1938)
(60) Churchill, *The Gathering Storm*
(61) *British and Foreign State*

Papers, Volume *cxlii* (1938)
(62) Churchill, *The Gathering Storm*
(63) *Hitler's Speeches*
(64) *Documents concerning German-Polish Relations* (H.M.S.O., 1939)
(65) *Ibid*
(66) *Ibid*
(67) *Hitler's Speeches*, II
(68) *Documents concerning Anglo-Polish Relations*
(69) *Documents on British Foreign Policy, 1919–39* (third series)
(70) *Documents concerning German-Polish Relations* (1939)
(71) *Nuremberg Documents*, II
(72) *Documents concerning German-Polish Relations*
(73) *Documents concerning German-Polish Relations and the Outbreak of Hostilities Between Great Britain and Germany on September 3, 1939* (H.M.S.O., 1939)
(74) *The Outbreak of War* (H.M.S.O., 1939)
(75) *Proceedings of the International Military Tribunal for the Far East, No. 216*
(76) *British and Foreign State Papers*, Volume *cxl* (1936)
(77) Herbert Feis, *Road to Pearl Harbor* (Princeton, 1950)
(78) *Ibid*
(79) *Ibid*
(80) *Ibid*
(81) *Nuremberg Documents*
(82) *Joint Committee on the Investigation of the Pearl Harbor Attack*, Washington, 1946, Part 20
(83) *Foreign Relations: Japan*, II
(84) *Ibid*

Further Reading

Avon, Lord, *Facing the Dictators* (London, 1962)

Beard, Charles A., *President Roosevelt and the Coming of the War* (New Haven, 1948)

Carr, E.H., *A History of the Bolshevik Revolution* (London)

Carr, E.H., *The Twenty Years' Crisis* (London, 1939)

Churchill, Winston, *The Gathering Storm* (Cassell, 1948)

Craig, Gordon, *The Politics of the Prussian Army* (Oxford, 1964)

Deutsche, Isaac, *The Prophet Armed: Trotsky 1879-1921* (London, 1954)

Earle, Edward Mead, *Makers of Modern Strategy* (Princeton, 1943)

Feiling, Keith, *The Life of Neville Chamberlain* (London, 1947)

Feis, Herbert, *Road to Pearl Harbor* (Princeton, 1950)

Fleming, D.F., *The Origins and Legacies of World War I* (Allen and Unwin, 1969)

Gaulle, General de, *The Army of the Future* (Hutchinson, 1940)

Hull, Cordell, *Memoirs* (New York, 1948)

Keith, Professor A.B., *The Causes of the War* (Nelson, 1940)

Kennan, George, *From Prague after Munich* (Princeton, 1968)

Nicolson, Harold, *Peacemaking 1919* (Methuen, 1964)

Rothfels, Hans, *The German Opposition to Hitler*, trans. Lawrence Wilson (Oswald Wolff, 1961)

Taylor, A.J.P., *Europe: Grandeur and Decline* (Penguin, 1967)

———, *The Origins of the Second World War* (Hamish Hamilton, 1963)

Thompson, David, *Europe since Napoleon* (Pelican, 1966)

Wheaton, Eliot B., *Prelude to Calamity* (Gollancz, 1969)

Wiskemann, Elizabeth, *Europe of the Dictators* (Collins, 1967)

Acknowledgments

The Publishers wish to thank the following for permission to reproduce the illustrations on the pages mentioned: the L.E.A., 8, 53, 54, 88, 92, 95; the Mansell Collection, 15 (*left*), 18, 23, 31, 46, 50, 59 (*right*), 66 (*left*), 69 (*left*), 70, 75, 76, 84, 91, 112 (*top and bottom left*), 115 (*left*), 121; the Radio Times Hulton Picture Library, 15 (*right*), 24, 25, 26, 27, 29, 32, 35, 38, 40, 53, 54, 59 (*top left and bottom*), 62, 63, 64, 65, 66, 69 (*right*), 78, 81, 87, 93, 100, 104, 106, 112 (*bottom right*); Keystone Press Agency Ltd., 66 (*top right and bottom*), 72; the Trustees of the Imperial War Museum, jacket; the Wayland Picture Library, 12, 115 (*right*).

Permission of the Controller of Her Majesty's Stationery Office has been granted for the extracts from the following, which are Crown Copyright: *British and Foreign State Papers*, vol. cxxxvi. 1933 (extracts 25, 26); *Documents on British Foreign Policy 1919–1939*, third series, vol. ii, ed. E. L. Woodward, 1938 (reports from Sir Neville Henderson, p. 90; minutes of the London Conference, 1938, p. 90; negotiations with Russia, 1939, p. 107.); *British and Foreign State Papers*, vol. cxii. (extract 4); *British and Foreign State Papers*, vol. cxviii. (extract 17); *British and Foreign State Papers*, vol. cxi. (extract 36); *British and Foreign State Papers*, vol. cxlii. (extract 61); *Documents concerning German–Polish Relations and the Outbreak of Hostilities between Great Britain and Germany on September 3, 1939*, Cmd, 6106 (extracts 64, 65, 66, 68, 70, 72, 73); *The Outbreak of War*, Ministry of Information, 1939 (extract 74).

Permission has also been given by Oxford University Press and the Royal Institute of International Affairs for extracts from the following: *Documents on International Affairs*, 1933 (extract 28); *Documents on International Affairs*, 1935 (extracts 43, 46); *Hitler's Speeches, 1932–39*, trs. Norman H. Baynes, 1942 (extracts 29, 42, 56, 63, 67).

126

Index

128